Bacardí

Hernando Calvo Ospina is a Colombian journalist, resident in Europe. He defines himself as being politically committed and this is reflected in his work. He has written various books, all of which have been translated into numerous languages. Among them are: *Perú: los senderos possibles* (Peru: The Possible Paths, 1994), *The Cuban Exile Movement: an exposé of the Cuban American National Foundation and anti-Castro groups* (Ocean Press, 1999) and *Salsa! Havana Heat, Bronx Beat* (LAB, 1995).

Bacardí

The Hidden War

Hernando Calvo Ospina

Translated by Stephen Wilkinson and Alasdair Holden

Preface by James Petras

Pluto Press

LONDON • STERLING, VIRGINIA

First published in French 2000 by EPO.

First English language edition published 2002 by Pluto Press
345 Archway Road, London N6 5AA
and 22883 Quicksilver Drive, Sterling, VA 20166–2012, USA

www.plutobooks.com

Author's email address: hcalvospina@hotmail.com

British Library Cataloguing in Publication Data
A catalogue record for this book is available from the British Library

Library of Congress Cataloging-in-Publication Data

Calvo Ospina, Hernando, 1961–
  [Ron Bacardí. English]
  Bacardí: the hidden war/Hernando Calvo Ospina; translated by
Stephen Wilkinson and Alasdair Holden; preface by James Petras. – 1st
English language ed.
      p. cm.
  Translation of: Ron Bacardí.
  ISBN 0–7453–1874–6 (hardback) – ISBN 0–7453–1873–8 (paperback)
  1. Bacardâi Corporation (Puerto Rico)—History. 2. Bacardí
Corporation (Puerto Rico)—Political activity. 3. Rum industry—United
States. 4. Rum industry—United States—Political activity. I. Title.
  HD9394.U54 B33313 2002
  338.7′66359′097295–dc21
                                                              2001006330

ISBN 0 7453 1873 8 hardback
ISBN 0 7453 1874 6 paperback

10   9   8   7   6   5   4   3   2   1

Designed and produced for Pluto Press by
Chase Publishing Services, Sidmouth, EX10 9QG
Typeset by Replika Press Pvt Ltd, India
Printed in the European Union by Antony Rowe, Chippenham, England

To:
Nabor Calvo, Elvia Ospina, Paula Andrea Calvo, Yohan Calvo, Karine Álvarez, Manolo and Alina, Miguelito, Annemie Verbruggen, Katlijn Declercq, Pedro and Odile, Miriam Rodríguez, Paquito, Luis Berois, Paco and Federica, Annette Lacoste, Alfonso and Rita, Enrique González, Teddy Gorman, Jaime and Leticia, Juan and Niurys, Florance Rigaud, Jesús and Miselda, Wanda Lawn. With special thanks to the Cuba Solidarity Campaign UK.

Without their support and kindness this work would not have been possible but that does not imply any legal responsibility on their part for its content.

All my operations are strictly carried out according to the American rules, and they always will be. This American system, which is our system, call it Americanism, call it capitalism, call it what you like, gives everyone and each one of us immense opportunities if we know how to grab them with both hands and squeeze them as much as possible.

Al Capone
Italian-American Gangster

Content

Prologue

by James Petras
Professor of Political Ethics at the University of Binghamton,
New York

This is the story of the close-knit relationship between major stockholders and directors of Bacardí rum, the extreme right-wing Cuban American National Foundation and the CIA. It provides a wealth of details documenting how Bacardí acted as a conduit for CIA funding to paramilitary mercenaries in Nicaragua, Angola and of course Cuba. But this is more than a litany of horror stories about a nasty multinational corporation acting with impunity against desperate people struggling to improve their lives.

This book raises fundamental issues about the relationship between multinational corporations and imperialist politics, about the instrumental use by the state of private corporations to serve state-directed terrorism. Fundamentally, this study argues that multinational corporations are not simply economic units pursuing market maximising goals but political units that are used by the state to pursue clandestine activities.

By focusing on the role of Bacardí in the formation of the Cuban American National Foundation (CANF) and its direct participation in influencing US policy towards Cuba, it raises the issue of how foreign corporate executives with an ideological axe to grind can make policy behind the backs of US citizens and against their interests. Because the fact of the matter is that Bacardí is not a US corporation though it controls US legislators and contributed to the financing of President Clinton's election campaign.

The Cuban American National Foundation and Bacardí are tightly interlinked as key representatives of Bacardí are on the board of directors of CANF. The policies of Bacardí/CANF have been a major impediment to any rapprochement between the US and Cuba. The fact that the President of the US Chamber of Commerce – the major business association in the US has declared it a top priority to re-establish economic ties with Cuba – tells us that Bacardí-CANF are increasingly isolated from major business interests in the US. Why then does Washington persist in following the extremist policies of Bacardí-CANF?

Calvo Ospina provides us with some promising leads to uncovering why a numerically insignificant émigré group, concentrated in one city of one state (Miami, Florida) can wield so much influence. Wealthy right-wing extremists provide up to 15 per cent of congressional campaign funds. More importantly, Cuban émigrés have played a major role in dirty clandestine operations in areas designated by Washington as being of strategic importance. Washington is loath to disown those who directed and funded the Nicaragua Contras, the UNITA mercenaries in Angola, the death squads in El Salvador or advised the fearsome political police in Chile. The Cuban émigrés are or have been a strategic asset.

Thus while an increasing number of major conservative US corporations and farm groups are clamouring for Washington to lift trade barriers with Cuba, the Clinton-Gore-Bush administrations resisted so as to avoid alienating their terrorist prodigy among the right-wing Cuban émigrés.

Calvo Ospina highlights the ideological terrorist component of US policy and the key role that Cuban émigrés and Bacardí played in implementing this policy. It remains to be seen, in this new post-Cold War era when the battle for the marketplace has intensified, whether Washington will opt for Bacardí or for the US Chamber of Commerce.

By Way of Introduction

(A)

Although they may not be facts well known to most people on the planet, it is not difficult to find information about unethical practices carried out by powerful transnational companies – practices that go against the interests of humanity, particularly in countries of the so-called Third World. Among the many such transnationals one could mention Shell, BP, Texaco, Total or Nestlé. However, when it comes to Bacardí, the world's largest rum producer, it seems that nobody has anything to say. Nobody dares to question this multinational which sells 240 million bottles (20 million boxes) annually of a spirit that is regularly consumed at parties in more than 170 countries.

Bacardí's name is scarcely mentioned in the world's media, despite the fact that in the middle of the 1990s, its lawyers helped to write a US law directed against Cuba and international trade, known as the Helms-Burton Law.[1] It was felt that this was just part of the ongoing confrontation between the United States and Cuba. As if it were normal that the leading, and only, superpower should tighten the noose around that small nation, just because its people had decided to be sovereign and socialist. A few months after the law was passed, Bacardí began a 'war' against the French-Cuban consortium Pernod Ricard-Havana Club Rum and Liqueurs, in a bid to remove its ownership of a brand name of rum. On this occasion the event was even less well broadcast, being relegated to the business sections of the newspapers. But Bacardí has a jealously guarded dark history.

(B)

It should be noted that in 1993, the Bacardí rum empire acquired Italy's Martini & Rossi, one of the world's biggest labels, for the fabulous sum of $1.4 billion. Thus it formed the Bacardí-Martini consortium, with headquarters in the tax haven of Bermuda.

Bacardí, the main house of the consortium, is a family firm that is not listed on the stock market. If it were, the shareholders would lose control of the company and 'the private details of the same would be aired openly'.[2] Founded in Santiago de Cuba in 1862 by a Catalan and a Frenchman, the shareholders took the most valuable asset of the company, the brand name, to the Bahamas a year before the victory of the Cuban Revolution. Since then, a good part of its financial activities has remained unknown, not only because of the advantages from being located in one tax haven, but also because another, Bermuda, is where the company has its central headquarters. However, what is known for certain is that the *holding* Bacardí-Martini (registered in Bermuda as Bacardí Limited) declared profits of $2.5 billion in 1999.

Bacardí has subsidiaries in Canada, Jacksonville, Miami, Mexico, Bahamas, Panama, Puerto Rico, the United Kingdom, Germany, Italy, France, Spain and Holland, where its European headquarters are located. These comprise 47 properties, 24 of them distilleries, the rest offices, and about 6,000 employees.

(C)

When you go abroad, for example to Chile or Morocco, and you see two vehicles passing by, say a Toyota and a Ford, you automatically relate them to Japan and the United States. They may have been assembled in Chile or Morocco but nevertheless you know that those trademarks do not 'belong' to those countries. A Phillips radio is Dutch, even if it is manufactured in Asia. Tequila is Mexican, even if it is bottled in Spain or produced in Guatemala.

But what about Bacardí rum? Some say it is from Puerto Rico, others from the Bahamas. The immense majority may not know why, but something makes people think that it is Cuban. Perhaps it is because Cuba is synonymous with rum. However, in Bacardí's case this is wrong because since 1960 no Bacardí rum sold anywhere in the world has contained even the slightest ingredient that comes from the island. Bacardí, the name, the trademark, is registered in the Bahamas, but the product itself does not have what might be called a homeland, a very unusual situation. This is not only serious for the rum's image, but also for its quality, because the sugarcane 'miel' (literally honey), as it is called, that goes to make the rum comes from canes harvested in several different parts of the Caribbean where the soils vary more than the climate. Thus the type of molasses produced from cane from the Bahamas is different from that from Puerto Rico. In spite of this, the 'miracle' of the markets and the shrewdness of its owners has turned Bacardí into the best selling liquor in the world.

(D)

This basic information has been included to help the reader to understand the context of a little-known subject: the *Hidden War* that Bacardí has carried out against the sovereignty of Cuba from 1960 onwards. But that is not all. Their policies have made them extend their arms much farther. This work is a mere introduction to the subject. There remains much more to investigate.

(E)

In May 1999, the descendants of the French Second World War hero and former President Charles de Gaulle wrote an open letter to a relative, also called Charles, a grandson of the general. This young Charles was standing as a candidate for the fascist National Front in the European elections. This so disgraced the members of the family, who do not share the views of National Front, that they made public their opposition.

The fact was that Charles the grandson had used the family name as a ruse in order to attract voters. The press release made clear that General Charles de Gaulle's political ideals had nothing to do with what his descendant was expounding. Therefore he was no longer able to be considered, not even tangentially, a part of the family.

(F)

The above-mentioned story is not gratuitous. The following investigation took a little more than a year and half to complete. As you will see, chief directors and shareholders of the transnational Bacardí have been involved, directly or indirectly, in secret as well as open political activity.

So far, the author has not found either a written sentence or a recorded tape in which any shareholder of the multinational expresses a disagreement with or a rejection of the facts presented here. And there are at least 600 shareholders, almost all of them part of the family. A few years ago, one of them, who in fact uses the Bacardí surname, was visiting Cuba to research the family history. Not even he is a critic of those who have plotted alongside the US government and groups of the extreme right in order to put an end to Cuba's sovereignty and destroy its Socialist revolution, let alone denounce the activities they have supported in other countries.

Since 1993, these shareholders have included the respectable Italian multinational Martini & Rossi and the directors of Pommery champagne, Dewar's Whisky, William Lawson's Whisky, Glen Deveron Whisky, Jack Daniel's, Benedictine, Southern Comfort, Bombay Gin, and other companies that are part of the consortium. Besides the fact that Martini is legally sold throughout the length and breadth of Cuba, so too is Jack Daniel's.

(G)

Finally, inevitably in such a complex situation, there will be many people and organisations which have links with each other. The author hopes that *Bacardí: The Hidden War* will reach a wide audience not necessarily specialised in the matter. For this reason, without compromising any investigative rigour, the book has been limited to dealing with only the absolutely necessary so as to make it accessible to all. Therefore, apart from very few exceptions, each name or event that is mentioned is implicated in or related in some way to the plot.

The author

1 The Bacardí-Bouteiller Company

THE SUGAR ISLANDS AND RUM

In the middle of the eighteenth century, the Spanish crown decided that Cuba would be the only producer of sugar in the empire, a decision which resulted in the proliferation of plantations of the sweet cane throughout the length and breadth of the island. The metropolis urgently wanted the white gold and in order to deliver it the extensive planting went some way towards damaging the fertile soil and the bodies of African slaves. The crown was blessed with good fortune. In 1791, Cuba was catapulted to becoming the world's leading producer and exporter of sucrose. It was in that year that the machetes of the Haitian slaves stopped cutting cane and began beheading their masters in the first mass rebellion of black slaves in history. A terrified rumour circulated among the gentlemen of the Caribbean, laying the blame for the diabolical insurrection on the consumption of rum. There could be no other explanation.

But after sugar came the rum. The Spanish crown used the mercantile trick known as protectionism to limit severely the export of Cuban spirit so that peninsular production did not have any competition. However, upon noticing the error, in 1796 that policy was radically changed. Cuba, with huge quantities of the raw material, took up the slack rope from its neighbours and began to attract French and English experts in making rum.

THE US ALMOST RUINS BACARDÍ

In 1830, attracted by the increase in trade with the eastern province of Oriente and keen to make a quick fortune, the Bacardí-Mazó brothers moved to Santiago de Cuba from the town of Sitges near Barcelona, in the old principality of Catalonia. According to the commercial register of the time, they set up a store in February 1841 where they sold provisions, hardware, clothes and spirits.[1] Three years later, the Sociedad Facundo Bacardí y Cía was registered as a clothing manufacturer.

Amid the abundance, when it was least expected, in 1857 the Cuban economy suffered a tremendous blow: the loss of markets in France and Germany which had begun to extract sugar from beet. At this point the United States took advantage of the situation to become the island's leading customer and impose its own terms of trade, including a spectacular drop in price.

It is certain that the Bacardís and other Cuban merchants cursed their bad neighbour to the north. Few of them survived total ruin, but among the survivors were the Bacardís. Their salvation lay in the fortunes of Lucía Victoria Moreau, who married Facundo Bacardí-Mazó, and another wealthy family the Arabitg-Astiés, who were committed to the Bacardís through being the godparents of two of them. With their financial support and spurred on by the stability of the price of rum during the crisis, the young José Bacardí-Mazó entered into rum production and sale.

BOUTEILLER PRODUCES BACARDÍ RUM

In June 1862 even the shade was no protection against the inclement sun that fell on Santiago de Cuba. But José León Bouteiller, who was of French origin, ignored the blazing heat and eagerly set out to teach the brothers José and Facundo Bacardí-Mazó how to make rum. Bouteiller was not the inventor of the distillation process. From times long past rum had been an integral part of the crimes, attacks and other diversions practised by the pirates and corsairs who roamed the Caribbean. Jamaica is the place most people believe the drink originated from, while Martinique, Haiti and other Antillian islands abound with fantastic stories related to the origin of this spirit that burns the throat and which made men of European adventurers.

On 24 February 1862, a transfer of property was signed in

Santiago de Cuba Town Hall. From that day onwards, the liquor company *Manuel Idral y Cía.* came to be called *José Bacardí y Cía.* A little later, on 2 June, the brothers José and Facundo Bacardí and José León Bouteiller went to the town hall in person in order to register their ownership of the company.

José Bacardí was the principal partner, having provided a capital of 3,000 pesos. Bouteiller, who had been ruined by the economic crisis and had been obliged to close his own distillery, transferred part of his equipment and became the second investor. Facundo, who had worked briefly for Bouteiller, borrowed a modest house (not part of the company's assets) with a large yard where the new business was set up to produce rum and other alcohols.

In general, Cuban manufacturers produced a good quality rum, but it was still too crude for the delicate palate and taste of the local and European aristocracy. Undoubtedly, the *Sociedad Bacardí-Bouteiller* spent great efforts on the improvement of its aroma and taste, especially Bouteiller who had much experience in the trade. It was a knowledge that Facundo quickly acquired, as he took part in the patient task of searching for the quality, the exact bouquet, that would distinguish Bacardí rum from others while it was still produced on Cuban soil.

In spite of the slow development of the company, Bacardí became nationally known on 10 November 1874 when Facundo, representing his wife and using her money as well as money received in inheritance from the Arabitg-Astié family, bought out his brother from the company. A month later, he showed Bouteiller the door and took over the distillery for himself, along with two of his sons, the Bacardí-Moreaus, renaming it *Bacardí y Cía.*

It is fortunate that the archives in Santiago de Cuba retain a mention of José León Bouteiller and his early support for Facundo. There are no records of him anywhere else despite the fact that without him there would never have been a rum called Bacardí.

EARNINGS THAT SOUND LIKE FANTASY

You get the feeling that the history of Bacardí in Cuba stopped with the disappearance of the first generation of its owners. The museum founded by Emilio Bacardí-Moreau, a patriot who fought against Spanish colonialism, is the pride of the inhabitants in Santiago de Cuba. The stories of the paternalism that the Bacardís showed towards the local population have been passed down orally through the generations. For this reason all the ruses that were used by those first businessmen in their rise to fortune have remained in the folk memory as picaresque anecdotes.

In 1880 a fire devoured the distillery and, with it, the archives of the company. But production was renewed a year later leading to earnings of 22,696.26 pesos in 1883. Inexplicably, between 1884 and 1890 it is almost impossible to find accurate information of earnings or losses. What is certain is that the company's balance sheet of 1891 showed assets of 64,839.45 pesos. Such high earnings are extraordinary considering that the company was still producing rum by hand. In 1899, the company's machinery and tools were valued at less than 6,000 pesos.

From 1891 to 1893 the accounts were all in the black, but then, surprisingly, the following year, and only in that year, losses were declared. At that exact time, the sons, Emilio and Facundo Bacardí, announced that they had a new partner, their sister's husband, Enrique Schueg. Their father, Facundo, had died in 1886. Enrique is still mentioned albeit only modestly by the official history of the company, almost certainly due to the continued though latent presence of his descendants among the shareholders. However, Enrique contributed an immense amount to the company with his solid capacity for commercial organisation acquired during his higher education in England.

BUSINESS AND PRO-ANNEXATIONISM

In 1898, when Cuba was about to achieve its independence from the Spanish colonial empire, the United States entered the war without any request from the Cuban patriots. Spain was defeated, but from 1901 the island became a US protectorate, meaning that it became a US semi-colony.

The first Cuban Constitution included an addition imposed by the US Congress called the Platt Amendment which recognised the right of the United States to intervene in Cuban internal affairs, limited the right of the Cuban government to sign treaties or obtain loans from abroad, and gave the United States the right to acquire land and run naval bases on Cuban soil. This degrading situation continued until 1933, although the basic principles of the amendment still remain in the relationship between the two nations.

But how does the transnational Bacardí-Martini describe today what happened in those years?

In 1898, United States forces helped Cuban patriots to cast off their colonial ruler and achieve independence, a process that had long been supported, at great personal risk, by the courageous contributions of Don Facundo's successor as head of the family, Emilio.[2]

Let's look at this more closely. The Emilio mentioned here is not the original founder of the Sociedad Bacardí-Bouteiller, but the son of Facundo and Lucía Victoria. Emilio Bacardí-Moreau did fight and was deported to Spain for fighting for Cuban independence. He was imprisoned on two occasions. But what does not appear in the official history of Bacardí is that, after his expulsion from Spain, the United States imposed one of their own military-like governors on Santiago de Cuba who in turn decided that Emilio should be mayor of the city. As an individual of principles who was loyal to the nation, he refused. He did become mayor and, later on a senator, but only after the Santiagueros elected him.

During those first years of the new century, Bacardí was one of the few native companies that made a profit from the semi-colonial condition into which Cuba sank. It was a situation that might be understood from the merely commercial point of view. What gives us cause for reflection is the way in which the matter is recounted by the multinational:

The US assisted Cuba in gaining independence, and Cuba, among its many gifts in return, gave North Americans a taste for the tropical spirit made in Santiago de Cuba: BACARDI Rum. In the climate of turn-of-the-century US protectionism, Bacardi thereby gained a foothold in a market that it would carefully cultivate.[3]

In 1910 the Bacardí company began their expansionist career by bottling rum in Barcelona. When the First World War exploded in Europe in 1914, Bacardí opened a distribution office in New York, thus making it a participant in the bonanza that the United States was enjoying at the cost of the European bloodbath. In 1913 its earnings had been 175,422.83 pesos, but as the end of the war approached in 1917 they had increased to 416,900.00 pesos.

There are numerous spurious explanations to explain the apparent incongruity between Bacardí's real productive capacity and its earnings in the early part of the twentieth century. For example, it is suggested that the company smuggled rum from Jamaica and packed it in Bacardí bottles to meet the demand. In Santiago de Cuba this is one of the past misdemeanours for which Bacardí is now forgiven; everyone there was happy with that generation of the family because, nationalists that they were, they reinvested their profits at home.

2 Expansion and Prelude to Departure

MILLIONS AMID THE CRISIS

In 1921, the company declared that its assets had amounted to about 6 million pesos in the previous year.[1] In 1927, the shareholders founded a brewery; in 1929 they began to bottle rum in Mexico and in 1936 they built a factory in Puerto Rico. Proud of their success and relishing the future, in 1936 the proprietors told the Cuban magazine *Carteles* that besides the above they also owned an immense distillery containing thousands of barrels of rum and a store of mature *aguardientes*. They said they could mature up to 5 millions gallons of rum. They also boasted of huge shipping warehouses, a box factory, another for bottles, another for producing ice, an electricity plant, several railway boxcars for the transport of their products, rail tankers for the transport of 'mieles' (literally 'honeys'), mechanical and carpentry workshops and a foundry; not to mention the magnificent Bacardí building in Havana.[2]

Due to its absolute dependence on the US, the economic crisis in October 1929 dragged the Cuban economy towards the abyss. But while the US recovered and continued along its resolute road, Cuba remained gravely wounded. In 1932, the price of the sugar fell to less than 1 cent a pound and the unemployment figures were worse than those of any other country. The rum barons were among the few members of the indigenous bourgeoisie who survived. Most struggled daily to keep their businesses against US competition. Their properties were fetching bargain prices for any foreigner.

From the Cuban commercial archives it is difficult to tell exactly what the Bacardí company did in order to achieve such a strong inventory. It is like looking for a needle in a haystack. In which bottle did the company hide its King Midas? Rum may burn, but it is not petroleum.

'THE RUM ROUTE'

In 1919, the US government passed the 18th Amendment banning the production, sale and import of all types of drinking alcohol. Prohibition, as it came to be known, opened the way to the formation of a new criminal class, initially known as bootleggers and racketeers, who later would evolve into the Cosa Nostra. Headed by people such as Al Capone, Santos Trafficante and Meyer Lansky, these gangs organised and developed the illicit production and smuggling of alcohol on a grand scale.

There were three key places where they could procure alcohol without much difficulty. These were three points on the map which, in the parlance of the criminal gangs, came to be known as the 'rum route': Jamaica, Cuba and New Orleans. By the time Prohibition was repealed at the end of 1933, the Mafiosi had converted themselves into powerful businessmen. The Cosa Nostra's millions washed through the US economy, leaving in their wake many gifts in the hands of not a few church dignitaries, politicians and security service chiefs.[3] That same year, Meyer Lansky received from the Cuban government the exclusive right to exploit the gambling casinos on the island. With this the Cosa Nostra succeeded in securing their 'first opening in the Caribbean, and the same would later happen in Nassau', according to the 'boss of bosses', Lucky Luciano.[4]

'THE GOLDEN AGE OF COCKTAILS'

What does the version of history published by Bacardí-Martini say about this period? What does Prohibition mean to its current shareholders and management? It should be noted that, just as Prohibition began, Bacardí rum was starting to gain prestige in the United States. Prohibition did not apply in Cuba:

The company grew rapidly in the new century. Between 1912 and 1919, sales increased. Then, in 1920, with the coming of

Prohibition in the US, history again dealt Bacardí an apparently telling blow which, characteristically, it turned into an opportunity. During Prohibition, all the famous international spirits were effectively excluded from the US market. However, Cuba, because of its proximity to the United States, became a prime destination for parched American vacationers. As they arrived in Havana, they were greeted at a bar that dispensed free Bacardí Rum cocktails. They continued to enjoy a variety of rum drinks all through their stay in Cuba in what has come to be known as 'The Golden Age of Cocktails'. North Americans returned home with happy tropical memories and a taste for Bacardí Rum. During this challenging period, although no sales were permitted, enthusiastic and inventive consumers found ways to bring Bacardí into the market against the restrictions of the law ...[5]

Let us keep in mind that prohibition not only filled the Cosa Nostra with dollars. When it was repealed, the official figures began to show that the sales multiplied for those companies that, directly or indirectly, had benefited from the illicit trade. Bacardí was among them. In the first year after Prohibition it sold 80,000 boxes of rum in United States.[6] How did Bacardí sell approximately 1 million bottles of rum so quickly in a market that had been closed for almost 14 years?

BUSINESS BEFORE NATIONAL INTERESTS

Bacardí's expansion was not without its critics at home. The Cuban economist and academic Jacinto Torras argued that the company's siting of bottling plants and factories in Mexico, Puerto Rico and the Virgin Islands was 'deeply harmful to the national economy'. For example, the processing plant in Borinquen, Puerto Rico, had an absolute logic for the shareholders because the rum produced there entered the US market tax free because the island is a US colony. Torras explained the matter in the following way:

> In order to defend their mercantile interests, the 'Bacardí' company often speaks of its 'Cubanism.' A very particular Cubanism that is carefully measured in pesos and centavos and very given to a keen hatred of the common interest [...] In the naked interest of business, mercenary to the highest degree [...] the current 'Bacardí' company denies in practice the pure Cuban history of Don Emilio [...]

The Cuban brand, having been born and credited in Cuba, and because it continues selling in the market of the north as Cuban, was taken to Puerto Rico and to the Virgin Islands, and this transfer marked a fall in Cuban exports of rum to the North American market. The source of work, taxes to the revenue, what the industry means for the national economy, the very feelings of Cubanism that could have existed, were no obstacle to this migration in search of a few dollars more [...][7]

There were millions of dollars, not just a few more.

BACARDÍ CONTINUES ON ITS WAY

A short while later, Torras returned to the attack against Bacardí's expansion which he saw as departing more and more from the Cuban national interests with each passing day.

With reference to a certain public debate that has been developing recently, Bacardí has lied again in seeking to justify the transfer of its factories to foreign countries. Bacardí has said that they have never stopped marketing rum from Cuba in the United States, but the statistics say something else. They say that the transfer of 'Bacardí' means that rum of Cuban origin has lost its pre-eminence among the imported rums to the United States, so much so that the pre-eminence has shifted to Puerto Rico. And to prove it, here are the statistics of the importation of rum in the United States from 1935 to 1940. They demonstrate that Cuba has been losing its position in the imports of rum [...].[8]

Using official data from the US Department of Trade, Torras shows that Cuban rum, which represented 52 per cent of imports to the United States in 1935, was reduced to a 7.3 per cent share by 1940:

Meanwhile, Puerto Rico increased the participation in the US import market of rums manufactured there from 14 per cent in 1935 to 64 per cent in 1940 and the Virgin Islands increased from 10.2 per cent in 1935 to 17.2 per cent in 1940 [...].

The official history of Bacardí acknowledges that at the beginning of the 1940s its businesses in Mexico and Puerto Rico overtook those located in Cuba.[9]

PEPÍN BOSCH EXPANDS THE BUSINESSES

While Prohibition in United States was still on, José Bosch, better known as 'Pepín', entered the Bacardí clan when he married the daughter of Enrique Schueg, one of the largest shareholders. He drew attention to himself by virtue of some unscrupulous business deals and was quickly installed in the company headquarters. In 1943, Pepín reopened the office in New York, thereby allowing the company to benefit later from the post-war recovery. Its merchandise was introduced into a flattened Europe almost as if it were part of the Marshall Plan. Distribution companies were started in Belgium, Switzerland, Sweden, Holland, France, Norway, Finland and Denmark. Because it produced rum in Puerto Rico, Bacardí was allowed to go wherever the great winner of the war went. Its tentacles even reached the Lebanon and Korea. In 1957, the company founded another distillery in Mexico with a capacity of 28,000 litres a day. The following year, a new plant was opened in Puerto Rico which doubled its production to 75,000 litres daily. In 1959, during the Franco dictatorship, Bacardí opened a distillery in Spain. Construction of a production plant began in Recife, Brazil, in 1960; while in Mexico and Philadelphia ...

TWO SHORT ANECDOTES ABOUT PEPÍN AND CO.

1. Pepín Hernández, the current director of the Rum Museum in Santiago de Cuba, recalls that in the 1950s Pepín Bosch proposed that the workers should become partners in a new company. He said that profits would be assured if they bought shares in *Minera Occidental* at a price of $10 each. By being a new company that would create employment, the law made it exempt from taxes on the import of materials and machinery. However, *Minera Occidental* dug a few metres of tunnel and was then declared bankrupt with most of the bankrupted stock of imported machinery and materials being bought by Bacardí. The most shocking part of the affair was the way in which those workers who had invested in the company lost all their money.

On his father's death, Pepín Hernández went with his share certificate, signed by Pepín Bosch himself, to try and claim their value. The answer that the strong man of the wealthy Bacardí clan gave was disconcerting. He told Pepín Hernández to bring him a letter signed by his father which proved that he was the rightful heir.

2. In February 1954, the child Facundo Bacardí Bravo disappeared. Although they were no longer admired as much by the 'common people' the members of the Bacardí family had not stopped being a fundamental part of Santiago society where the news exploded like a bomb. It was then that the Bacardís demonstrated some of their power, and the extent of their links with the US government.

The press of the time says that a search helicopter arrived a few hours after the disappearance. The aircraft had been despatched from the US military base at Guantánamo after Pepín had spoken with the US consul. Almost simultaneously, a plane arrived from Florida carrying an investigator from the FBI.

The search began. It was quickly discovered that two young workers belonging to the family were responsible. The boy was rescued within twelve hours. The first police reports said that the two kidnappers died in an armed confrontation with the authorities. It later became known that both had been unarmed.

'THE EMPIRE OF HAVANA'

With the end of Prohibition, Meyer Lansky, Number Two in the US Mafia, began to realise the potential that had been accumulated in Cuba during the previous decade. With the approval of the local bourgeoisie, to whom he gave grace and favour while they prospered with his dollars, he established 'The Empire of Havana'. Despite the fact that several important chiefs of the US security services had big investments in Cuba, the island became the leading centre in all the Americas for narco-trafficking, money laundering, organised gambling and prostitution.[10]

The Cosa Nostra ruled supreme in Cuba when Pepín Bosch became Minister of Finance under President Carlos Prío Socarrás (1948–1952). The Cuban state accounts flourished under his administration but he was part of a government that stood out because, in the words of Cuban historian Jesús Arboleya Cervera, 'Corruption and political banditry reached the category of official practice.'[11]

According to another historian, Enrique Cirules, Lansky had such a degree of influence in Cuba that, 'From the 1930s up to 1958 no political event of magnitude or any great business deal took place without the presence of his hand or attention. He was already doing business secretly or intervening visibly as a shareholder or consultant.'[12]

The Cuban state accounts flourished when they were administered by the man who was also president of the Bacardí company. It would not be untrue to say that this financial success was also in part due to the 'encouragement' offered by all the millions of dollars that arrived in the island via the Mafia.

3 Bacardí Leaves Cuba Before the Revolution

BACARDÍ MOVES TO THE BAHAMAS

In 1952, Fulgencio Batista ousted Prío Socarrás in a *coup d'état*, an act that certainly had the blessing of the Mafia and the US government, who saw in their man the possibility of uniting the disparate bourgeois political forces that were fighting over a share of the government. Washington's support for Batista lasted for almost six years, in spite of repeated official reports that defined Cuba as one of the leading centres of criminality in the world, including the traffic of heroin and cocaine.

Apart from thwarting members of the Bacardí family such as Pepín Bosch, who had been part of the Prío government, the coup did not affect the rum company. The millionaire's business did not stop, although a small but visible problem arose for Bacardí in 1957. An armed Havana university students' group tried, unsuccessfully, to attack the presidential palace. Many of the youths who survived the attack were savagely murdered in the ensuing days. Apparently, José Pepín Bosch did not agree with that wave of violence ordered by Batista and left the country in fear that the dictator would take reprisals against him.[1]

In fact, the manoeuvre was a pretext and the Bacardí boss soon returned, carrying some very special and valuable documents in his suitcase. These papers showed that the Bacardí company that had been founded in Santiago de Cuba had now relocated the world registration of its trademark in the Bahamas.

But why put the headquarters in the Bahamas, the favoured fiscal paradise of elusive and ill-gotten capital? Did Bacardí need to shield their accounts and transactions from the eyes of any authority? According to the company history, the transfer of jurisdiction was the assurance that the Bacardí Company had '[...] a safe harbour for its most precious possession, the trademark that bore its family name'.[2] Cuba remained the place that produced high quality molasses with which they made their rums. They kept their distillery in Santiago de Cuba as a marketing ploy because Cuba is a worldwide synonym for good rum. However, let's not forget that Cuba was also the place of the family's roots. But the trademark had been moved elsewhere.

All this happened before the arrival to power of Fidel Castro in 1959, and before the nationalisation of the company in 1960.

One of the stories told by the multinational suggests that it had begun to plan its departure from Cuba since the end of the 1920s, and for that reason had built the factories in Mexico and Puerto Rico. This was not only to evade Cuban taxes, but also because of the political uncertainty on the island. Coincidentally, Bacardí began to refer to this uncertainty at the beginning of the 1930s, exactly when the United States proposed the removal of the statute of protectorate over Cuba.[3]

A REVOLUTION INCOMPATIBLE WITH BACARDÍ

As Fidel Castro's rebel army advanced across the island in mid-December 1958, the US ambassador, Earl Smith, visited Batista to tell him that he should leave the government and the country, but before doing so he should install a junta with the responsibility of preparing elections. Smith even gave the dictator a list of the names of the chosen junta members. One of these was José Pepín Bosch.[4] The process of the revolutionary war had taken a turn for the worse and the US thought that the departure of Batista would help to have a steadying effect on the situation.

The dictator fled on 1 January 1959 without following orders. There was no junta and the guerrilla leadership assumed power. Bacardí's bosses, who had in fact contributed financially to that fight and convinced that its only goal was to put an end to the dictatorship, unfurled an immense banner on the facade of their building in Havana containing two simple words: 'Gracias, Fidel'.[5] The Bacardí family, and other members of the national bourgeoisie, were sure that by supporting the new regime they could displace national and foreign competitors. They thought that the revolutionaries would make some lukewarm social, economic and political reforms, but leave their privileges intact.

Carlos Franqui, a disaffected revolutionary published his version of several events that happened in those first years of the victory. In one aside he says:

> The first trip [of Fidel Castro] to the United States in April 1959 will be a masterpiece of political intelligence that will surprise the North Americans and will permit Fidel Castro to win time and prestige in the United States, in Latin America and Cuba.
> A high economic delegation accompanies him, including figures of prestige in the United States: Felipe Pazos, president of the National Bank [...]; Pepín Bosch and Daniel Bacardí of the noted rum firm, illustrious representatives of Cuban industry [...][6]

The fact that they accompanied Castro on this journey, and that they made the banner which thanked him, shows that Bacardí left Cuba for reasons other than the fear of 'future tyrannies'. One month later, in May, upon decreeing the first measures towards an integrated agrarian reform, the Cuban bourgeoisie, the US government and the Mafia realised that Fidel Castro and his 'Barbudos' (bearded ones) were going to fulfil their promises to the people. The changes in the offing were going to affect their interests, privileges and dreams in every way. This rang alarm bells in Washington as being a declaration of war, and President Eisenhower ordered the US forces to get ready for it. A group of those offended by Castro applauded the longed for decision.

THE NATIONALISATIONS WERE NOT A GAME

Law 851 was passed in July1960, granting powers to the Cuban president and prime minister to nationalise national or foreign properties when they considered it convenient to the defence of the national interest. The United States responded with an increase in terrorist attacks, and at the same time accelerating the preparations for the invasion at the Bay of Pigs.

The United States never recognised Article 5 of that law. This very clearly established the right of the expropriated to receive economic compensation. Republic bonds were created to pay the compensation 30 years later with interest through a special fund established at the National Bank. It was a fund that was yet to be filled because the nation's coffers had been emptied and transferred to the United States by many of the same people who were now lamenting the nationalisations. The law specified that the fund would be made up of 25 per cent of the revenues from the sale of sugar to the United States. However, this proved impossible because the US stopped buying Cuban sugar that very same month (July). The situation would be made worse on 7 February 1962, when President Kennedy officially established the economic, trade and financial blockade against the island.

The Cuban laws ordered the nationalisation of the Bacardí company. Nobody paid attention to the proposal expounded by the revolutionary government, which nevertheless abided by international treaties.[7] It was supposed that within a matter of weeks, months, or maximum one year, everything would return to normal. No one imagined that a government contrary to the US interests would survive for long. Years later, private or state companies of countries like France, Mexico, Switzerland, Great Britain and Canada decided that they did not want to carry on waiting and they accepted a settlement from the Cuban government. The US and Bacardí never have.

HOW THE REVOLUTION HELPED BACARDÍ

When the company and other properties of the Bacardí family were nationalised, a good part of the capital and goods were in other countries, including the trademark. The result was that the revolutionary government's action merely forced a technical adjustment of some minor details on the whole complex that existed on an international level.

Juan Prado, who was responsible for sales in Havana, played an important part in that adjustment:

> Prado was sent by Pepín Bosch to drum up business overseas with instructions to tell Bacardí's buyers that they would have to make a choice: Castro or Bacardí. Anyone doing business with Communist Cuba would not be welcome at Bacardí ...[8]

While they used this kind of threat against their clientele and potential buyers, in 1968 they set up a distillery in Nassau. This gave them the status of a domestic company and opened up the markets in the countries that were part of the British Commonwealth. There were other benefits, such as the ability to obtain sugar cane at preferential prices in UK colonies and protectorates in the Caribbean. Prado and another important Bacardí directors have acknowledged that, 'The whole experience of leaving Cuba [...] made the company less parochial and broadened its view of potential world markets beyond the United States and Latin America.'[9]

'The newly reformed company that emerged was no longer Cuban. Exile made it a company without nationality, long before the era of the multinationals.'[10]

4 The CIA, the Businessman and the Terrorists

THE BUSINESSMAN AND THE BOMBARDMENT

In the mid-1960s Bacardí's top boss decided to bomb the newly nationalised Cuban oil refineries. José Pepín Bosch was sure that if he left Cuba in darkness 'A state of national subversion would be created.'[1] His idea was not new. Cuban mercenaries in the pay of the CIA had been doing the same thing since the triumph the Revolution in January 1959.

Pepín bought an old B-26, by chance the favoured aeroplane of the CIA in its attacks against Cuba. Bacardí's boss took the craft to Costa Rica with the intention of launching the terrorist plan from there. Coincidentally, this was one of the countries that the CIA and their mercenaries used as a springboard for their attacks. The plane did not have rockets so Pepín went to look for some in Venezuela. He had no luck there. It seems that it was the Brazilian dictatorship who gave him two, but 'they did not inspire much respect'.[2] Everything was in place for a mercenary pilot to take off and set petroleum and human beings on fire. Pepín was to stay behind and wait for the results. Luckily, the bombing run was delayed: 'One morning, on the second page of the *New York Times* appeared a picture of nothing other than the said aeroplane.'[3] Facing a scandal, the government of San José asked for the aeroplane to be withdrawn, turning the plan into a short-lived adventure.

Similarly brief was the voyage of a ship given by Bosch to members of the Christian Democrat Movement who were determined to infiltrate Cuba in the early days of April 1961, just two weeks before the United States tried to invade the island at the Bay of Pigs with the mercenary Brigade 2506.[4] One of those on board the boat was José Ignacio Rasco, chosen by the CIA to lead the government (as a front) that would have assumed power if the Bay of Pigs operation had triumphed.

KENNEDY AND THE 'ORPHANS'

After the fiasco and humiliation of the Bay of Pigs, President John F. Kennedy decided to prepare another invasion, this time decisive and earth-flattening if necessary. He gave the green light to Operation Mongoose, an integrated operation that included economic asphyxiation and political work in order to isolate the Revolution internationally as well as ordering the US military to organise terrorism inside Cuba. As Kennedy said in November 1961, it was necessary to help the Cubans to overthrow the 'Communist regime', and establish a friendly government with which the United States 'could live in peace'.

Confronting such a threat, the government in Havana knocked on the door of the only country willing to give it heavy armaments, the Soviet Union. In October 1962, the United States alleged that nuclear weapons were being installed in Cuba, thus unleashing the famous Cuban Missile Crisis. They said that the world was on the edge of an apocalyptic conflict. But between them the powers solved the problem, and the Soviets made the US promise not to invade Cuba. But in spite of the pact, the essential element, that is, the invasion, continued to be at the root of US policy. It simply became necessary to make believe that it was the émigrés alone, 'orphans' of US help, who sought the 'liberation' of their country.

PEPÍN BOSCH PREPARES THE SECOND INVASION

During this period, Pepín Bosch decided to organise the counter-revolutionary émigrés with the aim of preparing a second attempt at invading the island. His plan was 'to gather a group of exceptional people, prominent men of the Cuban republic, and subject them to a referendum in order to create a world representative body of exiles who would be mandated to carry out actions in favour of the freedom of Cuba [...]'.[5] According to a memo of the National Security Council, the US government was aware of the plan.[6]

Bosch wasted no time in finding five 'exceptional people' who would be at the forefront of his plans. It is said that 64,000 families in the United States, Europe, and even Australia and Hong Kong registered to take part. Some 90 per cent voted for the Pepín's pre-selected quintet. So, at the beginning of 1964, the Cuban Representation in Exile (known by its Spanish acronym as RECE) was founded in Miami where the headquarters of the Bacardí company in United States was now located after having moved there from New York almost a year before.

Erneido Oliva, a former officer of Batista's army, was chosen as RECE's military chief. A man in the CIA's total confidence, he had been the second in command of Brigade 2506 at the Bay of Pigs. By a strange coincidence when he was called up to participate in RECE he had already been preparing for a second invasion for eight months. The training was carried out in the CIA base at Fort Benning, which specialised in courses on propaganda, covert actions, communications, espionage and secret operations.[7] The political chief of RECE was the lawyer Ernesto Freire. When the US government had to negotiate with its Cuban counterpart for the freedom of the thousand or so mercenaries captured at the Bay of Pigs, it chose William Donovan as the head of the delegation with Freire as his right-hand man.[8] Donovan is credited with having been among the main organisers of the US intelligence services.

Although he was not among those elected in Bosch's referendum, an almost unknown student leader of the Christian Democrat Movement called Jorge Mas Canosa quickly stood out in his role in charge of publications and public relations. After participating in the mercenary brigade – although he neither landed in Cuba nor took part in the combat – he was selected to go to Fort Benning where he was recruited into RECE. Tony Calatayud, another former mercenary in Brigade 2506, who was not voted on to RECE either, became one of its outstanding paramilitary activists and terrorists.

Thus the so-called 'democratic act', as Bacardí's boss had planned and called it, was annihilated because eventually it was Canosa and Calatayud, who alongside Freire, ended up as RECE's leaders, converting it into 'one of the strongest groups of its time'.[9]

CIA MONEY AND BACARDÍ

Given its proposed objectives, it was simply impossible that RECE would act without the blessing of the CIA. The agency had the responsibility, by presidential order, of directing and/or controlling all the threads of the counter-revolutionary spider's web. It has been said that the Cuban Representation in Exile was financed by their own means: 'Bacardí, gave the organisation $10,000 per month and paid each of the five leaders $600 per month, it was their primary source of income [...][10] However, it is difficult believe that such a large organisation with so many human and material needs could survive and develop sabotage and terrorist operations on a 'primary' income of $10,000 per month.

It is impossible to ignore the fact that they looked for other forms of financial support. For example, they used all the means of communication within their reach in Miami and other cities in order to appeal to émigrés. RECE declared that it was preparing a new invasion, but that it lacked money. The armed action would take place 'before the end of 1964, or, at the latest, before 24 February 1965'.[11] Many émigrés have testified that they poured dollars into this campaign. However, before long it was announced that the invasion had been postponed. The reason was never explained. And, according to some testimonies, the money evaporated. It is certain that a few years later it surfaced in investments in the RECE leadership's business portfolios.[12]

Official US documents uncovered by Congressional investigators also verify that the CIA financed RECE. In 1985, the FBI handed over a declassified document to members of Congress which revealed that the CIA station in Miami gave RECE money in order to increase its activities. In the same report, the FBI affirms that Mas Canosa and Freire were working for the CIA.[13]

Another FBI memorandum reveals that the agency gave Mas Canosa $5,000 to become a member of RECE. The money went to pay the expenses of a sabotage attack on a Cuban ship in the Mexican port of Vera Cruz. Planned in Fort Benning, the action was entrusted to a man called Luis Posada Carriles, who was at the time already a CIA special operative.[14] For a long time, Posada was RECE's chief of operations, turning it into one of the bloodiest terrorist organisations in the Western hemisphere.

THE PLOT TO ASSASSINATE FIDEL, RAÚL AND CHE

Although the document was made known to Congressional investigators in 1976, the National Security Council only allowed them to publish it in 1998. It was part of the investigations that

Congress carried out into the murder of President Kennedy and CIA plans to murder political leaders of other countries, in cahoots with the underworld, in particular the Cosa Nostra and many Cuban émigrés.[15] The letter that precedes the report reads:

> The White House
> Washington
> June 15, 1964
> Memorandum for Mr Bundy
> Subject: Assassination of Castro
>
> 1. Attached is a memorandum from the CIA describing a plot to assassinate Castro, which would involve US elements of the Mafia and which would be financed by Pepín Bosch.
> 2. John Crimmins is looking into the matter. He is planning to talk to Alexis Johnson about it and feels that it should be discussed in a Special Group meeting. John's own inclination is that the government of United States cannot knowingly permit any criminal US involvement in this sort of thing and should go all out to stop the plot. This would involve putting the FBI on the case of the American criminal elements involved and intervening with Bosch.
>   I have not yet thought this through and respectfully withhold judgment.
>
> Gordon Chase

To summarise, what did the attached eight-point document that the CIA officials gave to their boss say?

That Pepín Bosch offered to contribute $100,000 of the $150,000 that the people linked to the Mafia requested in order to assassinate Fidel and Raúl Castro as well as Che Guevara. The 'prominent Cuban exile' who had proposed the matter to Pepín also told him that it would not be so difficult to fulfil the plan because the hired people still had contacts in Cuba, due to their business relations. The names of the participants were not recorded. However, nobody wanted to investigate the details of the plot: 'The identities of the persons [...] and how they plan to proceed with this mission [...] make it fairly clear at the beginning that the Mafia was involved ...' And Pepín knew it very well. According to the same report, on 25 April 1964 everything was confirmed as ready to go ahead. The final comment was: 'We hope to have some good news for you between 20 May 1964 and 25 May 1964.' Point eight of the report to the CIA director reads:

> In late May 1964, a prominent Cuban exile who spoke with Jose 'Pepín' Bosch reported that Teofilo Babún and Eliseo Gómez (Cubans who were in the Mafia plot to make the assassination attempts) had a plan under way to murder Fidel Castro for $150,000. Bosch claimed that he had committed himself to provide $50,000 and that he was hoping he could get the balance of the money from the United States government or from other sources. Bosch indicated that he believes that a quick change for the better in the Cuban situation can be brought about only by the physical elimination of Fidel Castro and that his elimination is well worth $150,000 ...

All this is serious enough, but the report's conclusion verifies once again that Pepín had friendships and even the protection of senior figures in the CIA. This is something that is implied in the letter to Mr Bundy, the Special National Security Assistant to President Johnson, who was charged with relations with the CIA, a post he had also held under President Kennedy. Moreover, the report of Richard Helms, the director of the CIA, who was another of the magnates harmed by the nationalisations in Cuba, states: 'Note: It is requested that this agency be informed of any action contemplated in regard to the persons mentioned in this report before such action is initiated' (FBI 105–131629–5).

UNITY FOR TERRORISM

One of the most difficult tasks that the CIA had was to integrate the almost 400 counter-revolutionary cells and groups in order to facilitate their control and the development of their plans.

Fortunately, RECE and Bacardí marched as one. RECE proposed that the other groups unite, co-ordinate their actions and unify control. The authority that Pepín inspired, being who he was in the prestigious Bacardí company, facilitated the idea: 'Although there was already a proliferation of groups carrying out exile commando operations, in 1965 RECE began to co-ordinate disparate efforts, giving them a structure in which to operate.'[16] In the case of terrorist group Alpha 66, still for example, RECE maintained 'very good relations' with them, which still allowed them to discuss a potential financing of their activities in 1969.[17] From this unity of action 'emerged a movement of infiltration and armed attacks against the island that would occupy them to the end of the decade. They had ships, speedboats, of 25, 26, 27 feet in length [...]'[18]

At the end of the 1960s RECE proposed to stop the commando operations because all their men had either been killed in combat or were prisoners. Pepín Bosch and his people in RECE realised that 'in spite of all the resources gathered thanks to the relative freedom of the leaders of the organisation inside the United States and of their contacts in Cuba, they had not been able to even scratch the enemy'.[19] Despite this admission, Jorge Mas Canosa, the new leader of the Representation, sent a letter, dated 21 March 1969, to Proctor Jones, assistant to Senator Richard Russell, in which he says that the CIA 'could do much to contribute to an uprising inside the island, that would lead to the fall of Castro ... All that I request is logistical help in order to assist those inside Cuba who are desperately waiting for us to give them the weapons that they need.'[20] It is not known if he ever got a reply. What is certain is that 'on 12 March 1970, according to an internal memorandum, the RECE executive committee approved a credit of $600,000 for "warlike activities"'.[21] But where did all the money come from?

5 From Violence to the Lobby

ENTER JESSE HELMS

Jesse Helms of North Carolina entered the Senate for the Republican Party in 1972; if in February 1976 he found himself in Miami directing a speech to several hundred euphoric opponents of the Cuban government, it was because his political conscience was already that of a reactionary. Richard Stone, also a Republican senator for Florida, was another special guest at the gathering organised by the Cuban Representation in Exile (RECE).

They were not the only stars that shone that day. William Buckley, who was boss of the CIA in Lebanon in the 1980s, was also there. Also present was Lieutenant General Daniel Graham, who one month before had been director of the Intelligence Service of the US armed forces. Graham was also a special collaborator of the Heritage Foundation, a think tank created in 1973 that went on to become the vanguard of conservative thought that would govern that nation in the 1980s.[1] It was not by chance that these people became associated with RECE. Nor should it be assumed that simply through being the head of Bacardí, Pepín Bosch could have lifted the telephone or sent them an invitation to summon them there overnight. The reality is that the meeting was a kind of indissoluble marriage. Because all of RECE's guests, in their own way, never stopped carrying out or supporting activities against Cuba.

FROM THE BRAZILIAN DICTATORSHIP TO
THE CHILEAN DICTATORSHIP

In spite of having centred their activity on commando and terrorist attacks during the 1960s, the Cuban Representation in Exile and other groups tried to make contact with several Latin American governments looking for political legitimacy. RECE decided on Brazil, where the military had displaced the progressive President Joao Goulart in 1964 with the approval and support of the US government. Pepín Bosch and Representation leaders thought that the dictatorship, 'according to all political probability, should be inclined towards opponents of Castro'.[2]

The Brazilian dictatorship facilitated some things for the counter-revolutionaries. But giving them official recognition was not easy. Given the sympathies that the new Cuban government invoked in a large section of international opinion, no country dared publicly and officially to acknowledge them. With the exception, that is, of the United States.

However, in September 1973, an event took place in Chile that ricocheted around the world. General Augusto Pinochet carried out a bloody coup against the democratically elected Socialist President Salvador Allende. How he did it is already well documented; Nixon had given the order to prepare the overthrow, a task taken on by the Secretary of State and future Nobel Peace Prizewinner, Henry Kissinger. As in Brazil, the CIA, the multinational phone company ITT, the big information media, the trade unions influenced by the American Federation of Labour and Congress of Industrial Organisations (AFL-CIO) and the Christian Democrat Party paved the way to the dictatorship.

The Cuban counter-revolutionaries congratulated Pinochet. The Bay of Pigs Veterans' Association honoured him with the Medal of the Freedom. The association had good reasons for taking such an action, not only because they coincided ideologically, but because the dictator had assured them that he would make life as difficult as possible for the Cuban government in the Organisation of American States (OAS). And so as to remove any doubt about his intention, in November 1974, at an OAS meeting, Pinochet arranged for a group of émigrés to petition against Cuba's readmission to the OAS, from which it had been expelled in 1962.

But that public space offered by Pinochet would only be the modest face of the coin. The dictatorship began 'a special relationship' with some counter-revolutionaries, not only including them as advisers to his repressive forces, but facilitating weapons, explosives, training and refuge.[3] Among these counter-revolutionaries was the terrorist Orlando Bosch, a known CIA agent, who although without family ties to Pepín, was already involved in RECE.[4]

TERRORIST EFFECTIVENESS AND ECONOMY

At the start of the 1970s the international focus of the US government was the war in Vietnam where the guerrillas of the Vietcong had its powerful army on the brink of defeat. This implied a reduction of economic and political contributions from Washington. The 'Cuban problem' would have to wait.

Approved by the CIA, a replacement tactic took shape: terrorism pure and simple. A few men and less than $10,000 could be more effective than an entire commando mission.[5] In April 1974, a meeting took place in New Jersey to present what was called *La guerra por los caminos del mundo* (the war for the roads of the world). Among those presiding was RECE leader Tony Calatayud. It seems that Mas Canosa, the other leader of the Representation, was not present. However, the journalist David Poppe, of the magazine *Florida Trend*, stated in November 1974 that Canosa 'remained in contact with different terrorist operatives who were linked to what was known as the JM/WAVE alliance'. JM/WAVE was the code name of the CIA station in Miami under the direction of secret operations specialist Theodore Shackley.

'The war for the roads of the world' was translated into a systematic increase of bombs and murders in the whole American continent, Europe and even Japan. It was directed against Cuban diplomatic and commercial headquarters, the buildings and ships of countries with whom they traded, and even facilities of the UN. Judging by the diversity of attacks in so many countries so distant from their base, it would be reasonable to assume that the terrorists had the support of some great organisation (the CIA?). By themselves they would never have established the necessary logistics in order to explode a bomb, for example, in Madrid or Paris. In the French capital, a bomb explosion in the Cuban embassy in July 1974 was claimed by the Cuba National Liberation Front (FLNC in Spanish), a sinister umbrella apparatus of several groups among which RECE could be found.

COMPLICITY THROUGH SILENCE

In a bid to win the votes of Castro's opponents, President Gerald Ford went on the attack in the elections of 1976. He demanded that the revolutionary government should cease its solidarity with the Puerto Rican independence movement as well as pulling its internationalist troops out of Angola. This encouraged the gangs. On the verge of losing control of these, the CIA pressured the most radical factions to meet in the Dominican Republic in the summer of 1976. There they formed a coalition called the *Coordinadora de Organizaciones Revolucionarias Unidas* (CORU). The idea was the result of an order from the then Central Intelligence Agency director and future president, George Herbert Bush.[6] 'The main counter-revolutionary organisations existing at that time were incorporated into it and a key factor of inspiration and support for the meeting was the Chilean junta.'[7] Orlando Bosch, who was an adviser to DINA, the sinister Chilean political police, was chosen to lead CORU. Tony Calatayud remained in the nucleus of the leadership. Among those present were others close to the Cuban Representation in Exile, such as Posada Carriles.[8]

In August 1976, a bomb destroyed the car in which Salvador Allende's former Minister of the Interior, Orlando Letelier, and his US assistant were travelling. The horrendous crime happened in Washington but resonated politically throughout the country, prompting a broad investigation which concluded that several Cuban émigrés who operated for the CIA and the Chilean DINA were involved.

On 6 October, not long after the murder attempt, a Cuban Airlines plane was dynamited in mid-flight. The bodies of 73 people were strewn across Barbados. Eight days later, the Venezuelan authorities arrested Orlando Bosch and Luis Posada Carriles, who, we already know, were intimately involved in RECE. Posada Carriles had been sent by the CIA to advise the Venezuelan security forces, even reaching the position of commissioner of the political police.

No counter-revolutionary group, or any of their members, condemned that crime. On the contrary, some tried to justify it in various ways. The Bacardí family was one among many who remained silent.

National and international pressure forced the US government to take action against the most recalcitrant elements. 'The war for the roads of the world' was abandoned. It had not managed to destabilise the Revolution and in fact had produced a feeling of repulsion among the majority of the people of United States. It was now time to direct resources towards another strategy. Political work, in suits and ties, through corridors and offices, was the direction to take. The visit of Jesse Helms and associates to Miami marked the turning point.

As the Cuban émigrés' historian, Álvaro Vargas Llosa, puts it: 'RECE wedded itself to rum and politics again, and Bacardí was put in charge once again of almost all the bills [...]'[9]

WOLVES IN SHEEP'S CLOTHING

José Pepín Bosch, guided by his powerful US establishment connections, sent the ambitious Jorge Mas Canosa to knock on doors in Washington. On his way, Mas Canosa met Frank Calzón, a graduate of the conservative University of Georgetown. Calzón was an outstanding militant of Abdala, an organisation founded by a 'veteran of the "Cuban Units" of the United States' Army'.[10] Abdala acted as the political wing of the Cuba National Liberation Front. In 1975, the 'abdalistas' created an organisation called Of Human Rights, of which Calzón was made executive president. Parallel to this, practically single-handed, he ran another lobbying body called the Cuban American Public Affairs.

Also in 1975, Richard Stone presented a resolution in the Senate to stop tourism to Cuba. That was not all. He diligently promoted the creation of a committee of colleagues in favour of a 'Free Cuba', to which counter-revolutionaries would contribute $250,000. According to Vargas Llosa, 'Thanks not so much to this respectable endowment as to the fact that there are still North American anti-Communist politicians, 17 senators agreed to include their names in this attempt to use the institutions of democracy in order to influence policy.'[11] Pepín Bosch's financial contribution was substantial. What remains difficult to establish is to what extent Stone and the other senators who joined 'Americans for a Free Cuba' participated in this. Among them was Jesse Helms, who not only signed the resolution but decided to give it a bit of a boost.

6 Reagan Breeds a Monster

GOODBYE RECE, HELLO CANF

In 1988, the official break-up of the Cuban Representation in Exile was announced, although in fact since the early 1980s RECE had only existed as another acronym in a plethora of counter-revolutionary groups. From 1981 onwards, several directors and shareholders of Bacardí, old leaders of RECE and several operatives of the CIA got together and built a super-modern structure: the very focused, economically powerful, politically and ideologically ultra-rightwing Cuban American National Foundation (CANF).

In order to understand how the CANF is linked to the political and economic interests of Bacardí, it is first necessary to understand its basis.

THE NSC AS FATHER AND MOTHER OF THE CANF

From the moment that Ronald Reagan won the election, Richard Allen, who would become one of his main external security advisers, suggested involving the Cuban émigrés in his plans.[1] The counter-revolutionaries had proved their loyalty to US needs, above all military and paramilitary, in several places around the planet.

The suggestion was accepted, but one pitfall had to be overcome. The terrorist activities that the émigrés had carried out against the Cuban Revolution and, in quite a few instances, their relationships with the drug traffickers made them vulnerable to public opinion.[2]

So the search began for people whose image was not so tarnished. It appears that twelve men were called to meet with Allen. The majority had been either members of the CIA, closely co-operating with it, or in the service of other secret US units. All had achieved an acceptable reputation in conservative intellectual, managerial and business sectors. Apart from the participation of some in the ill-fated Bay of Pigs invasion, their past was not involved directly in serious criminal activities.

It was revealed some time later that one member of the National Security Council (NSC) told them that if they improved the image of the Cuban émigrés, they would get help to do something for the 'freedom of Cuba', by introducing them to the political leadership.[3] This is how the Cuban American National Foundation was conceived at the heart of the Reagan administration in July 1981.

The Foundation was established as tax-free non-profit association with 'scientific, educational and charitable purposes'. Taking Allen's advice, it was structured along the lines of the powerful Jewish lobby, the American-Israeli Public Affairs Committee. That is to say, with a wing entrusted to work for political influence in the state apparatus, effectively the CANF itself, and a supposedly independent Committee of Political Action, whose function was channelling economic contributions to politicians without compromising the rest of the organisation.

The former member of Abdala (FLNC's political wing), Frank Calzón, was the first executive director. When he renounced the post a little later, Jacqueline Tillman took the position until 1992. As if to prove the roots of the organisation, Mrs Tillman was formerly a member of the National Security Council. Meanwhile, the Cuban-American intellectual, José Sorzano, did the opposite to Mrs Tillman and passed from the executive of the Foundation to the NSC.

'PROJECT DEMOCRACY'

The involvement of the extreme Cuban right wing in the strategy of the Reagan administration was consolidated in January 1983 when the president signed Directive No. 77. This secret plan would become known inside the select National Security Council as 'Project Democracy'. One of its central objectives was Central America, where burning social problems had produced the politics of insurrection. It was small and poor Nicaragua, with its nascent and popular Sandinista revolution, which was the primary target. It was number one on the list because it was regarded by President Reagan as a threat to the national security and the foreign policy of the United States. Logically, Cuba did not escape the plans, being considered the main instigator of the situation and acting under the presumed orders of the Soviet Union.

'Project Democracy' had two faces. The first was military and secret in character, far away from the supervision of Congress. The co-ordination of the operation was given to Lieutenant Colonel Oliver North, veteran of the special secret operations developed in the wars in Indochina.[4] The second, despite its public character, was supervised by an expert in propaganda of the highest circles of Special Operations of the CIA. This was called the National Endowment for Democracy (NED). It was formed as a non-governmental non-profit corporation. However, its funds were (and continue to be) approved in the federal budget, under the gaze of Congress.

The NED grew and gradually became the favoured instrument of US intervention policy, taking on tasks that, until then, had been carried out by the CIA in a covert manner: penetrating non-governmental organisations in detailed medium- and long-term projects.[5]

THE CANF AND 'PROJECT DEMOCRACY'

One of the first tasks of the CANF was to participate in the anti-Sandinista crusade that was carried out inside the United States as much as it was in Central America. In this way it became an important appendage of 'Project Democracy', to the point of being one of the most important receptacles for dollars distributed by the NED. According to Vargas Llosa, 'The daughter of Reagan's "Project Democracy", the National Endowment for Democracy [...] put resources into the hands of numerous Latin American groups, among them the Foundation and several other exile organisations.'[6]

According to the congressional investigator Gaeton Fonzi, the Foundation received several million dollars from the NED during the Reagan and Bush Sr administrations; that is to say, between January 1981 and January 1993. A large amount of that money was only in transit, destined to finance other activities, like the Reagan's secret war in Central America.

At least until the end of the 1980s, US security services and the

White House participated directly in the decisions of the Foundation. Its leaders had to attend regular meetings where members of the security services provided information on the situation in Latin America and passed on instructions for the Foundation to follow.[7]

According to Fonzi, Raúl Masvidal, one of the principal directors of the CANF, 'In retrospect [...] didn't realise' that the Reagan administration had set up the Foundation 'not to specifically advance the Cuban cause but as part of a larger scheme'. 'Not initially,' he says, 'but after you've been burned two or three times by the machinations of the CIA and the US government, you get skeptical.'[8]

THE FIRST GODFATHERS OF THE CANF

Among the NSC characters who set up the Foundation and also worked for 'Project Democracy' was the CIA Director, William Casey, who, Vargas Llosa says, 'had an affectionate relationship' with the extremist émigrés.[9] There was also the academic and ideologue Roger Fontaine, who had been entrusted with Latin America on the NSC. Fontaine is a member of the World Anticommunist League (WACL) and of the Center of Strategic International Studies (CSIS) of the University of Georgetown, the home of US neoliberal thinking. Another key character in the development of the CANF was Robert McFarlane, the instigator of the Contra insurgency against the Sandinistas and one of the editors of the so-called Santa Fe Document.[10]

On the other hand, the politicians Jesse Helms and Richard Stone invested substantial efforts in Congress to get acceptance and support for the CANF, as did Dante Fascell, a Florida Democrat who presided over the Foreign Relations Committee at the time. Jeanne Kirkpatrick, wife of a former high official of the US intelligence services, also supported the CANF for many years.[11] Mrs Kirkpatrick, an influential personality in the Heritage Foundation, Freedom House and other conservative institutions, as well as being Ronald Reagan's ambassador to the United Nations, was appointed to the CANF Advisory Council, where she shared a seat with the politician Richard Stone and none other than Bacardí's José Pepín Bosch.[12]

7 The CANF and the Shareholders

Because their interests coincided with the aims the Reagan administration had for the Foundation, it wasn't long before more than 100 Cuban businessmen resident in the US joined its board of directors. Each was prepared to make an annual contribution of between $5,000 and $50,000. Many were linked in one way or another to US counter-espionage services, mainly the CIA.

In addition, the potential influence that this group could wield within the community in Florida, its ability to bring to bear economic resources so crucial in the US political landscape, and its relationship with the commercial and political sectors both within the US and overseas made it vital to the cause.

BACARDÍ'S DIRECTORS STRENGTHEN THE CANF

Within the Foundation this business group has always represented a significant influence 'in the wings'. Various shareholders from within Bacardí joined right from the Cuban American National Foundation's inception. No other business or family group has been so widely represented on such a permanent basis in this kind of 'sanctuary' for the extreme counter-revolutionary right.

These shareholders have been among those responsible for instigating every kind of legal, undercover and other activity launched by the Foundation since 1981. They have formed an integral part of the group of directors taking decisions, approving proposals and putting them into practice in favour of US interests, primarily in its war against Cuba.

This is not to mention numerous members of the family belonging to the Foundation as 'Associates'. Although they cannot be elected to the board of directors they assume all other rights, responsibilities and privileges, including participation in the General Council. This requires a minimum annual contribution of $2,000.

Amongst the most prominent members of the Bacardí family who have formed part of the governing council of the Cuban American National Foundation are: José Pepín Bosch, Clara María del Valle, Gerardo Abascal, Lourdes Abascal Quirch, José Bacardí and Manuel Jorge Cutillas (see Appendix).

Pepín Bosch had given up his managerial position in the Bacardí company in 1976. He remained, however, one of the most significant and influential shareholders. Until his death in 1994, he shared the table of the CANF Advisory Council with the likes of Senator Richard Stone, Jeanne Kirkpatrick, William C. Doherty and Peter Grace: these last two were also governors of the American Institute for Free Labor (AIFL), an AFL-CIO regional organisation. Both of them along with their labour 'organisation' have been exposed as having close links with the CIA.[1]

For their part Cutillas, Abascal, Abascal Quirch and José Bacardí have served on the CANF Board of Trustees alongside a whole range of Cuban-Americans, including, as fate would have it, the ex-head of Cuban Representation in Exile and one time US secret serviceman Ernesto Freire.

It was in the mid-1980s that Clara María del Valle, the maternal granddaughter of a Bacardí, became involved in the Foundation's activities. She acquired decision-making powers from 1989 with her accession on to the board of directors, becoming executive vice-director in 1999.

There are also important members of the Bacardí family who, whilst not enjoying membership of the Foundation's executive, have provided contacts, assistance and/or financial contributions. Amongst these are Juan Prado, Juan Grau, Rodolfo Ruiz, Eduardo Sardiña and Edwin Nielsen Schueg, all high-ranking executives in the company.[2]

THE ROLE OF CONSERVATIVE INTELLECTUALS

Intellectuals and diplomats in the Cuban American National

Foundation also warrant close examination. Although few are to be found on the governing body, there are many who play a part in the advisory group. Those most highly valued are mainly linked to the Heritage Foundation, Freedom House or emanate from the Catholic University of Georgetown. Together with Frank Calzón, other eminent personalities include José Sorzano, Ernesto Betancourt and Luis Aguilar León, editor of *El Nuevo Herald*, who has eulogised the Bacardí Company in his newspaper.[3] They, along with their circle, shared ideas, activities and exchanges with intellectuals from other countries. Foremost amongst these were Fernando Arrabal, Carlos and Jorge Semprún, Philippe Sollers, the British historian Sir Hugh Thomas, Mari Paz Martínez Nieto, Mario Vargas Llosa, Bernard-Henry Lévy and Jean-François Revel.[4]

In the case of France, the first meeting took place in 1979 with Revel, Lévy, Arrabal and Sollers as the main participants. In October 1991 another similar meeting was held in the French National Assembly to coincide with the opening of the Fourth Congress of the Cuban Communist Party. This was co-ordinated by Eduardo Manet, resident in Paris, and Carlos Alberto Montaner, resident in Madrid. Its principal goal was to persuade the French and Spanish governments to recognise the legitimacy of the main exile groups. The role of presiding over this event fell upon Mario Vargas Llosa who had already lent his support to the US blockade against Cuba[5] and the meeting was 'organised by the French review *La Règle du jeu* of the anti-Marxist philosopher Bernard-Henry Lévy'.[6]

Following the collapse of the former Soviet Union, in April 1992, as the imminent disappearance of the Cuban revolution was being mooted, another meeting was held in Paris. This was organised once more by Montaner and Manet, with Revel and Lévy lending their full support. It included an energetic contribution by the émigré Néstor Almendros, who a few years previously had released his CANF-subsidised documentary *Nadie escuchaba* (Nobody was listening).[7] It was also attended by leaders of the Foundation as well as other representatives of extremist organisations based in Miami such as Hubert Matos and Ricardo Bofill. The meeting was held in the Centre de Hautes Études sur l'Afrique et l'Asie Moderne (Centre for Advanced African and Modern Asian Studies) '[...] under the auspices of the office of the Prime Minister, Edith Cresson'.[8]

ACADEMIC INFILTRATION

As the result of the similarity of their ideological viewpoints, the links between the Foundation, the Center of Strategic International Studies of the University of Georgetown (CSIS), the Heritage Foundation, Freedom House and Miami University were strengthened. In addition the Foundation was to grant important financial assistance to the CSIS and Miami University which was to become more than a straightforward academic relationship.

At the end of the 1980s the Cuban American National Foundation created the Endowment for Cuban Studies (ECAS) whose main objective was to produce documents of political analysis and to encourage activities concerning Cuba in academic centres and universities. An example of this was the way in which the Endowment for Cuban Studies together with the University of Miami organised a series of meetings to debate relations between Cuba and other countries, just as Europe was witnessing the collapse of the socialist bloc. Invitations were primarily extended to politicians, diplomats and intellectuals from the USSR, Poland and Hungary.

As can be guessed the principal characters within the ECAS leadership were drawn from the above-mentioned conservative institutions: Jean-François Revel, Jeanne Kirkpatrick, Hugh Thomas, Luis Aguilar León, as well as Mario Vargas Llosa, and so on.[9]

The activities of the Endowment for Cuban Studies were centred on the Center for Cuban Studies of the University of Miami, and with very good reason. At the beginning of 1990 the Foundation made a proposal to the Florida International University (FIU). As the faculty of the same name was supposedly dominated by the left, it wished to set up the Endowment for Cuban Studies to run parallel to it. This Endowment, in which every state dollar would be matched by a dollar from the Foundation, would award scholarships and fund conferences, studies and publications. However, a significant number of students and tutors rejected the proposal, fearing the loss of academic independence.

The conflict was to take on a national dimension which was to reach its climax in 1991 when the Florida State Congress authorised the creation of the Endowment but for the University of Miami. This establishment had up to that time been almost completely dominated by the reactionary émigré faction. Congress also pledged a sum of $1 million, thereby forcing the Foundation to contribute an equal sum. According to Álvaro Vargas Llosa, 'The Foundation raised the million dollars in the blink of an eye – Bacardí made a significant contribution – and that's how the Endowment for Cuban Studies was born [...]'[10]

THE 'BACARDÍ CHAIR'

There was a somewhat bizarre precedent to the Center for Cuban Studies. In 1986 the Emilio Bacardí Moreau Chair, better known as the 'Bacardí Chair', was created at the University of Miami. Figures linked to the Foundation and Bacardí, such as Luis Aguilar León, Irving L. Horowitz and Jaime Suchlicki, were invited to give lectures on themes central to the post such as 'The History of Cuba and Understanding Cuban Culture'.

As a matter of fact, Bacardí boss Manuel J. Cutillas has been the president of the International Advisory Board of the University of Miami.[11] Note that the advisory board of a centre of higher education is headed by 34 executives representing banking, commerce, industry and the media. According to the university's publicity the group works with the rector 'to develop programs of international studies and student recruitment together with advancing the Center for Cuban Students'.

RADIO MARTÍ

Although approved as early as 1983 along with 'Project Democracy', it was not until May 1985 that broadcasts of Radio Martí aimed at Cuba began. The intellectuals, politicians, sympathisers and supporters of the Cuban American National Foundation were now able to broadcast their theories and exhortations directly at the island. The delay was due to strong opposition from a significant section of US Congress that believed it to be ineffective as part of a strategy to undermine the Cuban government.

According to the main interested parties the station signified 'the Foundation's first important act in collaboration with the US government'.[12] In the National Security Council, Richard Allen pushed for its creation. It was ironically named to carry the name of José Martí, the Cuban who had struggled most for independence against Spanish colonialism and who had foreseen the US's desire to annex his country. Again Allen could count on the assistance of those who had been in favour of the creation of the Cuban American National Foundation: Jesse Helms, Richard Stone, Dante

Fascell, Robert McFarlane and Jeanne Fitzpatrick among others. In addition Allen and the exiled extreme right had the support of a key man: Charles Wick, head of the main US propaganda machine, the United States Information Agency (USIA).[13]

Hilda Inclán of the News Department left Radio Martí 'accusing the directors of violations of federal laws and irresponsible journalism'. At the same time 'she complained that the investigative section of the broadcasting company was an intelligence apparatus [...] As a matter of fact the investigative section had become the backbone of the radio station.'[14] Rolando Bonachea, director of the station, expressed the following during a lecture in the Institute of Cuban Studies (ECAS) of the University of Miami:

> Currently Radio Martí [RM] and TV-Martí [TVM] are the biggest centres for investigation and information regarding Cuba. Whereas the CIA has only three analysts of Cuban origin dedicated to these types of investigation and the Defense Department only two, RM and TVM have 220 employees totally dedicated to the study of Cuban current affairs together with government activities both inside and outside Cuba.[15]

Radio Martí began with an annual budget of $14 million, and this figure has increased gradually year by year. In spite of this it has not achieved its primary objective of inciting the uprising of the Cuban people against their government. Concerned by the situation, several important Bacardí directors and shareholders joined forces with 'Citizens for a Free Cuba', a group of prominent conservatives from Cuban American and US political circles. In an open letter to President Clinton, among other things they pleaded for 'the intensification of transmissions to Cuba by Radio and Television Martí and other communications channels with the aim of informing and motivating the people'.[16]

8 Two Wars and their Accomplices

The Fall of 'Project Democracy'

On 6 October 1986, an aircraft was shot down by a patrol of the People's Sandinista Army. Documents found on the only survivor, the US citizen Eugene Hasenfus, proved what the Nicaraguan government had been saying unheeded all along: that the White House was directing an illegal and terrorist war against its territory, using the so-called Contras as the mercenary means of achieving its goals. Days later, on 25 November, the US Attorney-General revealed that money made as a result of the illegal sales of arms to Iran had been diverted to finance the Contras war. Reagan and his government were not just to weather a storm as a result of these revelations: a whole cataclysm was to descend and become known as Iran-Contragate. Public opinion was at a loss to understand how Reagan could sell arms to the Ayatollah Khomeini through Israeli intermediaries while at the same time condemning him as a 'terrorist demon'. Furthermore, the cash (a total of $36 million in two years) was being channelled into financing acts of aggression against a country with which America was not officially at war. More revelations were being made day by day, uncovering a series of secret activities which were in violation of human rights, US law and Congressional dispositions.[1]

The final straw came when it was proven that the anti-Sandinista operation had also been financed with cash proceeds from drugs trafficking. Cocaine and marijuana supplied by the heads of the main Colombian drugs cartels to one of Project Democracy's networks were transported to airfields in Costa Rica, Honduras and El Salvador along CIA-controlled routes. From there the drugs were airlifted to civil and military airports which another network would control market distribution.[2] In return, the Colombian criminals received arms, sophisticated security equipment and assistance to ease access to the US market for their own shipments. It is a certainty that the Colombian Mafia would never have become what it is had it not taken part in the Contras war.[3] At the same time, Reagan convinced his 'fellow Americans' and almost the whole world that his government was waging a war against drugs.

What the media had begun to uncover was further revealed by Congressional investigations, headed by the representative, John Kerry. In their obsessive war against Nicaragua, Ronald Reagan and his team had dragged the nation into an act of 'state banditry'.[4]

Public Means, Private Means

Through the CIA and the National Security Council, William Casey, Robert McFarlane and Oliver North launched an umbrella organisation called the Nicaragua Freedom Fund. This instigated and co-ordinated in large part the efforts of a wide range of private right-wing organisations. These organisations afforded and sought political and practical assistance both inside the US and elsewhere, including the collection and transfer of funds to the Contras. Their principal public figurehead was Jeanne Kirkpatrick.[5] The terrorist Posada Carriles, adviser to the mercenary forces, observed that, 'The CIA, in charge of this project, were very much in favour of an independent group providing assistance to the Contra rebels with arms and ammunition [...]'[6]

As had been anticipated from its creation by 'Project Democracy', the National Endowment for Democracy was put in charge of shifting millions of dollars destined for the mercenary Contras through these organisations. For its part, the State Department directed the United States Agency for International Development, (US-AID), the US Information Agency and other agencies within its remit to co-ordinate the delivery of supposed 'humanitarian aid' to the mercenary forces. However, the Congressional inquiries uncovered that this public and private aid was merely a cover for the purchase and provision of US military aid and supplies.

Moreover, the involvement in drugs trafficking was found to go all the way up to the State Department, given that various organisations and operations under its auspices were used for it.[7]

With the Freedom Fighters

The Cuban American National Foundation played a direct role in the whole of this anti-Sandinista operation. This would include those shareholders and heads of the Bacardí multinational, who are involved in the organisation's decision-making process.

Until the early 1990s the Foundation took no pains to hide or disguise its role as an agent of US foreign policy. On the contrary, its real nature was expressed unambiguously: 'We support President Reagan's initiative to lend moral and material assistance to freedom fighters in Cuba, Afghanistan, Ethiopia, Cambodia, Nicaragua, Angola and other countries [...]'[8]

Its leadership had no hesitation in announcing its involvement in operations: 'Our active participation in the Central American conflict and our efforts to inform and guide those who have pledged their allegiance to the cause of a Free Nicaragua cover a whole range of activities [...]'[9]

And if any doubt lingered regarding the connection of the Foundation to this 'dirty war', one only has to read Álvaro Vargas Llosa, who was very close to it: 'The origins of this collaboration are to be found in the closing stages of the first Reagan administration, when Theodore Shackley, ex-CIA joint Director of Operations and head of the Secret Services Section, requested that members of the Foundation helped in Central American policy [...]'[10]

Let's not forget that according to declassified FBI documents, it was the CIA base in Miami, under Shackley, that maintained relations with and delivered substantial aid to Cuban Representatives in Exile: the paramilitary organisation created by the head of Bacardí, José Pepín Bosch.

The Principle of Brotherhood

Among the many things brought to light by Iran-Contragate was the presence of Luis Posada Carriles in the Salvadorian base of Ilopango, a key strategic military enclave in the Central American war. Posada Carriles had escaped from a Venezuelan prison where he had been imprisoned for his part in the blowing up of a Cuban Airlines plane in October 1976. He had paid $28,000 dollars in bribes to make good his escape.[11]

According to an article in the *New Republic* published in 1985, this money was raised by the leaders of the Foundation. In his autobiography, Posada Carriles states that in August 1985 he landed directly in Ilopango: 'Unbeknown to me Félix Rodríguez, alias Max Gómez, a brigade comrade [from the Bay of Pigs], was waiting for me at a military airfield on Salvadorian territory.'[12] Rodríguez was not unknown. A veteran of special operations in Vietnam, he was implicated in the assassination of Che Guevara after having helped to capture him in Bolivia in 1967 on the orders of the CIA. A close friend of ex-President Bush, he walks into the headquarters of the Foundation as if it were a second home.[13]

What was Posada Carriles up to in Ilopango? He says: 'I took part in supply operations from El Salvador, with flights almost daily to Nicaragua organised by Air Force Supplies, financed and controlled from Washington by Oliver North.' He also throws light on who was to take care of his needs the moment he arrived at the base: 'A group from Miami, very highly placed people, among them Jorge Mas Canosa, Feliciano Foyo, Pepe Hernández and others, have made the effort to sort out my financial needs [...] Every month I'm sent enough money [...]'[14]

It is possible that the Bacardí bosses and shareholders, although they were prominent Foundation members, knew nothing about the activities of Canosa, Foyo and Hernández. Nevertheless, it is clear that the executive directors of an organisation to which they belonged financed a known terrorist.

AID TO UNITA IN ANGOLA

The Civil War in Angola

In 1974, Portugal gave up the last remnants of its colonial empire. The following year, it left Angola in the midst of a brutal civil war which it had itself stoked up. The US and the apartheid South African government came to the aid of the National Union for the Independence of Angola (UNITA) which was on the verge of defeat by the People's Movement for the Liberation of Angola (MPLA). UNITA could also rely on the support of Germany's Christian Democrats as well as the French centre parties.[15] Facing these military, logistical and political disadvantages, the MPLA requested assistance from the Cuban government.

However, the US presence in Angola was not to consist of regular military personnel but of undercover military operations launched mainly by the CIA. It had a clearly defined strategy: roll back the MPLA in order to exacerbate political, social and ethnic divisions, thus triggering a civil war which, irrespective of the ultimate victors, would leave Angola bloodied and weak with UNITA the only alternative to chaos.[16]

In 1975, the CIA together with other US and European secret services began a huge campaign of 'psychological warfare'. Disinformation was disseminated in the world's media telling of the wholesale destruction of settlements or the rape of women by Cuban soldiers. Simultaneously, as the US trade union confederation AFL-CIO pressed on with the organisation of trades unions against the MPLA, some 200 radio stations, newspapers and press agencies – among them AP, UPI and Reuters – were flooded with propaganda, financed wholly or in part by the CIA, as uncovered in the findings of a US Senate investigation.[17] The CIA campaign was successful in 'that a large number of intellectuals, "independents", "neutrals" and other noteworthies' collaborated in their psychological warfare project; many of whom were ignorant of the manipulation in which they played a part.[18]

In 1976, the US Congress approved the Clark Amendment which outlawed the supply of arms or military aid to either side in the conflict, for fear of provoking another Vietnam. But, just as was to occur with Nicaragua some years later, Congressional directives were not adhered to either by the White House or the National Security Council.

Pepín Bosch, the CANF and UNITA

In the US the press agency Black, Manafort, Stone and Kelly was given PR responsibility for promoting the image of UNITA and its leader, Jonas Savimbi.[19] This same consultancy also contributed to the setting up of the Cuban American National Foundation in the 1980s. It was only logical therefore that it would end up being an important link between UNITA and the Foundation.[20] It set up a meeting between the two organisations with the approval of the National Security Council and the State Department. The plan was to sidestep the Clark Amendment by helping private organisations (the Heritage Foundation was at the forefront of those chosen) to do their dirty work.[21]

According to NSC thinking, the situation in Angola represented the balance of power between the capitalist and communist blocs, a continuous process following the end of the Second World War

– in other words another chapter in the Cold War. The heads of the Foundation, along with the entire anti-Castro Cuban American population, saw the Angolan conflict as an opportunity of a showdown with the Cuban government as it had posted several thousand troops and advisers by order, according to the US, of the Soviet Union.[22]

According to the Foundation biographer, Vargas Llosa, the Black Manafort, Stone and Kelly Studio was given a budget of $600,000 and 'the job of controlling the image of Savimbi in the US; and the Foundation and Pepín Bosch took charge of the running costs of the Angolan organisation committees in various US cities [...]'[23]

As an instrument of US foreign policy, the Foundation was another organisation which dedicated itself to the repeal of the Clark Amendment. As a result of the various activities and pressures brought to bear by the lobby, the amendment was repealed in July 1985, thus authorising the release of millions of dollars and the sending of heavy arms to UNITA. Senators Larry Smith and Dante Fascell played a crucial role in this. Fascell, an old acquaintance of the Foundation, also happens to be a head of Black Manafort, Stone and Kelly.

Agreements with UNITA

On 28 January 1986, Jonas Savimbi arrived in Washington to a hero's welcome from conservative politicians and groups, becoming the most renowned of 'freedom fighters' in the process.[24] By this time, UNITA had been transformed by its allies into a powerful military force which, although unable to destabilise the Angolan government due to lack of internal political support, had managed to commit thousands of atrocities against the civilian population.

By now relations between UNITA and the Foundation, including the Bacardí shareholder members, were closer than ever. This was to be made clear in a public announcement by the CANF:

> Our ties with Jonas Savimbi and UNITA, his visit to the US and the material aid he is currently receiving from this country show the success of the Foundation's efforts in properly educating and informing US public opinion.[25]

Towards the end of March 1988, a committee of the executive and other members of the governing council of the Foundation arrived in Jamba, the 'capital' of UNITA-held territory. On 1 April a joint declaration was signed, the most important sections being:

[...] having realised a wide-ranging and profound dialogue on the struggle by the Angolese (sic) for their freedom and the close links which said struggle maintains with the cause of the Cuban people [...] it has been resolved:

1. That the quest for liberty, democracy and dignity in Angola and Cuba constitutes a common cause amongst both peoples; [...]
3. Consequently the Cuban American National Foundation undertakes to participate actively in a campaign at global level and particularly in the US with the aim of promoting UNITA's just cause [...]
5. That following the advent of peace and dignity in Angola through national reconciliation, UNITA is committed to providing its determined efforts to assist the Cuban people until liberty and democracy are restored in their country.

UNITA and the Cuban American National Foundation reaffirm their total commitment to the cause of human rights and democratic principles.[26]

Aid to Criminals

More than ten years were to pass following the signing of this joint declaration. A peace treaty was signed between all warring parties and in 1989 Cuban troops began to leave Angolan territory. Yet neither UNITA nor its allies were to respect this peace accord nor any other international agreement. UNITA, with a great military capability that is even yet to manifest itself in the political arena, has continued to spill the blood of the Angolan people. This genocidal army has caused hundreds of thousands of crimes and refugees and is still led by Savimbi, supported by the US and tacitly supported by European states: this is so because of the huge diamond, iron and oil extraction operations along with the strategic position of this West African region. The condemnations of UNITA by the United Nations seem to be lost in a bottomless pit.

In 1999 the following warning was published:

Wanted. This man is a war criminal. He has murdered thousands of Angolans, destroyed homes, public places, schools and hospitals; stolen millions of dollars with his diamond smuggling; used mercenaries to assault Angola and keeps thousands of civilians in a prison regime. He is financed by all those who wish to see the dismemberment of Angola.[27]

Who are we talking about? Jonas Savimbi.

It is not known how long Savimbi and UNITA benefited from the campaign to clean up his image in the US. It cost hundreds of thousands of dollars, a fair amount of which, let us recall, was handed over by the Foundation and the Bacardí magnate, José Pepín Bosch.

9 The Torricelli-Graham Act

HERE'S TO THE FALL!

In 1989, as the fall of the so-called socialist bloc was being anticipated Washington was investing in plans to speed up its demise. The National Endowment for Democracy, for example, distributed millions of dollars to private organisations – already mentioned various times in this book – for them to invest in the Soviet Union, Poland and Romania. Their task was to bring influence or pressure to bear in targeted areas; to create and lend support to so-called 'independent' human rights groups and newspapers and so forth; and to 'finance dissidents and other activists'.[1]

The Cuban American National Foundation was called upon to play a crucial role among all these groups. What was going on in these countries was to have a profound effect upon it. This was to result in its wealthy chiefs, among them those from Bacardí, together with the NED going on to finance and implement a strategy devised by the National Security Council and the State Department. This was primarily to apply pressure on the Soviets so that they would break all economic and military links they still held with Cuba. This plan found favour with US politicians Connie Mack and Robert Graham (both directors of the NED), Dante Fascell and Larry Smith. Mack and Smith accompanied the CANF leaders to Moscow with the aim of meeting high-ranking government officials to discuss the subject. In exchange for ditching Cuba they offered the Soviets preferential relations with political and economic sectors in the US, particularly in Florida.

The CANF and US strategists in the war against the Cuban government got what they wanted. On the morning of 25 December 1991 a delegation from the CANF held a meeting with the new Foreign Affairs Minister of what had already become Russia, Andrei Kozyrev. The minister 'promised to put an end to subsidies and change the relationship with Cuba to one strictly based on commercial lines: in other words, to buy and sell goods at market rates, to speed up the withdrawal of troops and to vote against Cuba in Geneva'.[2]

'That was when the glasses were raised to toast a free Cuba. Because in a way that morning sealed Castro's fate. That was when the halting of economic aid to Castro was announced to the world [...]'[3] 'There was nothing secret about the discussion. We raised a toast in front of the TV cameras with Bacardí rum.'[4]

The box and bottle stood out in the middle of the table, the name of the rum displayed for all to see. The Bacardí multinational had secured a big slice of the cake for its expansion and future conquest of this enormous market, and had been given an added boost thanks to images of the toast being given prominent coverage on television and in the press. At the same time in a besieged Cuba, a period of scarcity comparable to that endured by the inhabitants of several European countries at the end of the Second World War was about to begin.

'IF BLOOD HAS TO FLOW ...'

All this formed part of a well-structured, long-term policy. At the very beginning of 1990, the CANF's chairman, Jorge Mas Canosa, distributed a document intended for the directors only. In it are 'laid out the tactical elements which will be implemented prior to the expected collapse of the communist government' (see Appendix). Given the Foundation's subsequent behaviour one can conclude that the proposed actions contained in the eleven pages of text were approved by the governing body. Given that Bacardí shareholders formed part of this exclusive nucleus, below are some paragraphs which assist in revealing the true nature of their human and political conscience (italics are the author's).

> Use to the full *the political and economic agreements made with the CANF* by the chairman of the House Committee for Foreign Affairs, Dante Fascell, and fellow Congressmen and women Connie

Mack, Larry Smith, Ileana Ros-Lehtinen and others, in order to bring before Congress those items which will strengthen Castro's international isolation and hasten the fall of tyranny [...]

Form a Task Force to *systematise links* with the National Security Council (NSC), the Central Intelligence Agency (CIA), and the Federal Bureau of Investigation (FBI) in order to guarantee, with the utmost urgency, the identification of a policy and measures to be taken against the Stalinist Cuban government, *a greater exchange of intelligence data and economic assistance* necessary to bring our plans into being [...]

Organise a task force to systematise and strengthen working relations established with the State Department with the aim of jointly *devising and developing new international policies* which respond to the current situation [...]

Nothing nor no one will make us falter. We do not wish it but if blood has to flow, it will flow.[5]

This is how the document, written on official CANF paper, ends. Its letterhead lists the names of all the directors, including for example José Bacardí, Manuel Jorge Cutillas, Clara María del Valle and Gerardo Abascal, all Bacardí shareholders and bosses of Bacardí.

A LAWMAKER'S PRICE

'The last Stalinist dictator is about to fall only 90 miles from our shores [...] No power on earth will help him escape.'[6] This was how the New Jersey Democrat Congressman Robert Torricelli expressed himself in front of a selected audience in Florida in January 1992 as a guest of the Cuban American National Foundation. Yet what had happened to Torricelli? Why such a radical political turnaround in the same Torricelli who four years earlier had visited Cuba with the idea of reconciliation, who was a fervent critic of Miami's Cuban émigrés and an opponent of Radio Martí and aid to the Contras?

One cannot ignore the fact that the imminent demise of the isolated Cuban revolution had its effect: it is so obviously preferable to be alongside those who might be in power again. This was in keeping with a characteristic so typical of the US and one which the heads of the CANF learned to use to great effect: what is known as political 'horse trading'. It is unclear whether candidates to the Senate and the presidency have acted according to conscience when angling for the Cuban American vote in Florida or New Jersey. Though important this is it not the overriding reason; what is most important is the economic power wielded by the voters who are financial sponsors and are basically CANF sympathisers. Although in population terms the Hispanic vote in Florida represents only 7 per cent of the national total, their monetary contribution to electoral campaigns was 15 per cent of the national total in 1992.[7]

While many of the politicians who receive financial benefits are not from the Cuban-American community, the incentive remains the same: 'When an exile outlines his cause to a Congressman whose electorate have shown no particular interest of any kind in the Cuban question, and in passing offers to bolster his finances, it isn't too difficult to convince the Senator or Representative.'[8]

Those Bacardí shareholders who are also members of the CANF, along with others resident in the US or Puerto Rico, are noted for their contributions to Democratic and/or Republican candidates, depending on the interests at play, although with a predilection for the latter.

For its part, between 1980 and 1990, the CANF contributed $100,000 to electoral campaigns, part of this sum being money received from the National Endowment for Democracy. During this period the candidate receiving the largest amount was Dante Fascell. Torricelli received $27,750 from the Foundation for the 1992 electoral campaign, one of the sums which made him a political convert and standard-bearer of the opposition to the Cuban revolution, as highlighted by the US press.[9] These dollars, and possibly so-called 'soft money' that is given under the table, were an investment which would bring handsome dividends for the Cuban-American extreme right as Torricelli was made chairman of the Subcommittee of Western Hemisphere Affairs of the crucial Foreign Relations Committee.

WHY AND HOW A LAW IS PASSED

Like Torricelli, Representative Robert Graham was convinced that the Cuban revolutionary government would collapse at any moment. Already a long-standing ally of CANF, from the beginning of the 1990s he redoubled his efforts on its behalf whilst taking every opportunity to team up with other extremist groups.

Graham was the first to breathe life into the AFL-CIO's creation the Pro-Free Cuba Labour Committee, while reminding the organisation of the worthwhile efforts it had made in assisting the Polish Solidarity trade union. In a memo intended for the president of the AFL-CIO and also signed by his fellow politicians Dante Fascell and the Cuban American Ileana Ros-Lehtinen, he said: 'We are united with you in the hope that the AFL-CIO can play a similar role in Cuba.'[10] The AFL-CIO, a main beneficiary of NED subsidies in 1991, proposed that, along with other actions, it should smuggle literature into Cuba and make broadcasts on Radio Martí. At the same time, with Graham's blessing and as part of the campaign the AFL-CIO took up the cause of two convicted terrorists of the Alpha 66 organisation serving jail terms in Cuba.[11]

On 3 February 1992, Robert Graham announced to the press that the Torricelli Bill would from that week formally be known as the Torricelli-Graham Bill. Following this, Graham undertook a series of visits to counter-revolutionary organisations and newspaper offices in Miami to explain the bill. On each of these visits he was accompanied by a head of the CANF.[12]

During this time in Congress a press briefing was held in which Torricelli explained that the bill had been prepared to put even more pressure on Fidel Castro's government and to establish an 'infinity' of ties between Washington and Havana following his defeat. The bill, he said, was like 'a powerful signal to the regime in Havana that the US is determined to establish democracy on the island'.[13] It was presumably one of life's little coincidences that in another press conference on the same day in the same city some CANF chiefs were explaining the bill to another group of well-known figures, politicians and news media.

ELECTORAL OPPORTUNISM

President George Bush was not in favour of the bill. He had announced that if passed by Congress he would refuse to sign it, in spite of prophesying on 24 April 1992 that without the support of the former socialist countries of Europe Fidel Castro would fall quickly and that this would enable him to be the first US leader to visit the 'free soil of Cuba'.

Then the CANF adopted an intelligent approach. The country was in the midst of an election campaign, a time when anything can happen in this country where everything can be bought and anyone is prepared to compromise themselves to support the most outlandish and dangerous national or international policies. They approached the candidate Bill Clinton, who without having read the bill and just by blurting out in public the simplistic 'I like it' galvanised the Miami crowds, left many Congressmen on tenterhooks and Bush with a brain-teaser. Clinton travelled the Cuban neighbourhoods in Miami, reiterating his support for the bill and raising dollars for his election campaign.[14]

In response, President Bush sent a letter to the House of Representatives expressing his support for the bill. In a parallel and opportunistic way, and pre-empting the bill's progress in the House he used his executive powers to order the enactment of some of the sanctions contained in the Torricelli-Graham Bill. On 23 October 1992, Bush travelled to Miami. In the Hotel Omni, surrounded by various members of the Cuban American National Foundation and accompanied by heads of business and industry, he signed the cynically titled Cuban Democracy Act.

THE EFFECTS OF THE ACT

Senator Connie Mack was not on his own in ensuring that the bill became law although it is more than likely that he was the third person behind it. Previously, in 1991 he had presented an amendment intended to prevent overseas-based subsidiaries of US companies trading with Cuba which was subsequently incorporated into the Torricelli-Graham Bill. When President Bush signed the Cuban Democracy Act, one of the first statements made by Mack was: 'He [Castro] has to know that we are going to remove him from power by tightening the trade embargo. More importantly, [the Act] outlines and establishes the rules of the game governing the period of transition in a Cuba without Castro.'[15]

However, not all Cubans were in agreement about the Act. 'Some exiles argued that it was a new Platt Amendment, intended to control the destiny of Cuba following the overthrow of Castro.'[16] Congressman Charles Rangel, a New York Democrat, called it 'an abortion of an idea from the Cuban exiles who yearn for the days of the dictator Fulgencio Batista'.[17] Something which applies to those Bacardí shareholders, inside the CANF, who supported the law.

The three quotes mentioned above highlight the two central objectives of the advocates of the Torricelli-Graham Bill.

The Act became the focus of international controversy from the moment it began to be talked about in February 1992 and not just as a result of being an act of kicking a country already down on its knees. Europe and Canada, primarily, registered their discontent, as the Act did not respect international trade conventions. The attempt to prevent US subsidiaries in third countries trading with Cuba was the most contentious aspect. Canada and the UK quickly passed laws making it an offence to obey the US law, thus placing some US companies' overseas subsidiaries in a Catch-22 situation. The Act prohibited them from trading with Cuba while foreign laws prevented them from obeying mandates from the United States. Pam Chappel, spokesperson for the Canadian embassy in Washington, stated: 'The United States is the only country which attempts to extend its long arm beyond its own borders.'[18] At the United Nations, the United States attempted to justify the Act by claiming that the 'Castro regime' was a threat to its security and that it should therefore try to overthrow it. This justification was thrown out by almost all the member states who perceived the Act as legally unacceptable due to its extra-territorial provisions affecting the sovereignty of other nations, its unilateral extension of measures interfering with the freedom of trade and movement, and its advance in protectionism on behalf of US products.[19]

Faced with a barrage of criticism, the US government attempted to freeze or water down the most controversial aspects. Meanwhile, Torricelli, in overbearing mood and revealing expansionist desires, a trait seemingly common to all those who supported the Act, proffered the following:

Canada and Mexico sold out to Cuba in order to proclaim their independence from the US based on a crazy notion of sovereignty. But Cuba is not China; it's smaller, less powerful and lives in the shadow of the US [...][20]

10 The Absurd: The Helms-Burton Act

JESSE HELMS AND DAN BURTON

> Let me be clear: whether Mr Castro leaves Cuba in a vertical position or a horizontal position doesn't matter to me. That's up to him and that's up to the Cuban people. But he must, he will leave Cuba.[1]

These are not the words of Robert Torricelli. Three years after the passing of the Torricelli Act, in even more aggressive fashion, this is a statement from the most reactionary senator ever to enter the US Congress, the Republican Jesse Helms.

The 'tobacco senator', as he was known due to his connections with the Philip Morris multinational, is an old friend of the Cuban-American extreme right. His connection goes back as far as 1972, when José Pepín Bosch, the Bacardí magnate, and his Cuban Representation in Exile invited him to give a speech during a demonstration in Miami.

On numerous occasions from the moment it was brought into being, Helms has manifested his agreement with the CANF. In addition, South and Central American dictatorships and repressive governments have all enjoyed his open and committed support. The disdain in which he is held by the majority of the people in these poor countries is understandable given that he stated that the overseas aid given by his country was akin to 'throwing it on to a rubbish tip'.[2]

Dan Burton, a Republican from Indiana without a high school education, became a Congressional Representative thanks to financial assistance from the business sector. Along with the ex-military chief John Singlaub, Burton headed the executive board of the National Defense Council Foundation. This think tank, created in 1978, promoted itself as researcher and adviser on the 'advantages' of the so-called 'Low Intensity Conflict'. This counter-insurgency strategy was put into practice in various Latin American countries, even where no guerrillas were present, and had as its central aim the repression of the civilian population. Representative Burton has also been a member of the Conservative Caucus, a foremost centre of reactionary thought, on whose governing council he has served along with Jesse Helms, together with the ex-high-ranking military chiefs Daniel Graham and John Singlaub. Burton achieved global notoriety in 1991 when he called for the atomic bombardment of Iraq during the Gulf War.[3]

THE COBBLED TOGETHER ACT

Dan Fisk, a member of the Heritage Foundation, who had been working in the Department of State and on the Republican Party's Foreign Affairs Committee, joined Jesse Helms's office as an adviser. In 1994 the first and just about only task given to him was to revise all the anti-Cuba bills that other members had recently presented before Congress; and in truth there were more than a few.[4] Fisk quickly put together all of Torricelli's proposals together with those of the Cuban-Americans Lincoln Díaz Balart, Robert Menéndez, Ileana Ros-Lehtinen and other legislators.

In tandem, Fisk was charged with fronting a special task force to align itself to the chief aides of these politicians and those of Dan Burton, Robert Graham and Connie Mack.[5] A series of meetings were subsequently organised with a complex yet precise aim: to produce a bill from the bits and pieces of the other bills.

In December 1994, the first version of the bill called euphemistically 'The Democratic Solidarity and Liberty for Cuba Act' emerged from Jesse Helms's office. In the following two months it underwent numerous redrafts, mainly written by Washington and Miami lawyers assisted by Fisk's group. These lawyers also happened to be working for an esteemed private client who would benefit enormously from measures in the bill were they to become law.[6]

58   Bacardí

THE BATTLE COMMENCES

At the end of January 1995 it was public knowledge that the Congressmen supporting the Helms-Burton Bill had close ties with the Cuban-American extreme right, primarily as a result of payments into their election coffers. In February, Helms held a press conference to present the bill; this was his first important initiative as president of the influential Senate Foreign Relations Committee. With Senator Helms by his side, Robert Graham reiterated that, 'We have an obligation to our principles and to the Cuban people to elevate the pressure on Castro until the Cuban people are free.'[7]

From that moment, a long and arduous battle would commence from which few would emerge unscathed.

President Bill Clinton expressed his reservations in spite of his favourable stance towards the CANF during his campaign for the White House. There is no doubt of course that he initially failed to realise the extent to which they would go and he was now forced to face up to the folly of electoral opportunism. If the Torricelli-Graham Act gave him a headache with his European allies and especially Canada and Mexico, the Helms-Burton Act could have thrown him into an absurd and unnecessary series of worldwide legal cases. Moreover, Clinton now recognised that the Act aimed to create within Cuba a 'pressure cooker' without an escape valve. This was a concern shared by some important US interests which, while not in agreement with the Cuban political system, concluded that the implementation of the Act would result in catastrophe on their doorstep. It would deepen the misery of the Cuban people and increase the chance of unrest and violence sparking the intervention of Cuban-Americans and possibly the US. 'A nightmare scenario', according to the *Washington Post*.[8]

The President's backtracking prompted Senators Helms and Mack to make a public statement, the most pertinent extracts of which were:

This week the US Senate has reacted to reports that your Administration was considering proposals to reduce the pressure on the Castro dictatorship, scrutinising the Cuban Liberty and Democratic Act [...]
If you really are thinking about weakening the US stance towards Castro's regime we respectfully warn you that we are against this. We will oppose you by any means at our disposal.

If you are not contemplating such a change you are almost certainly obliged to say so immediately and in clear terms. The most effective way to eliminate any doubt regarding your views is to lend your support to the Democratic Solidarity and Liberty for Cuba Act [...][9]

THE BATTLE REACHES EUROPE

In April 1995, the Helms-Burton Bill was approved by the House of Representatives Sub-Committee for Foreign Relations in the Western Hemisphere, chaired by Dan Burton. In its bellicose report, without any political justification, Burton stated that to negotiate with Fidel Castro was like 'working with Stalin, or Hitler, or Ceaucescu or Honecker'. Burton went on to bluster: 'Businesses that are ignoring our embargo, and dealing with Fidel Castro, will lose their shirt when that country becomes free. They need to realise this ...'[10]

During his presidency Clinton made great play of his lack of authority and credibility when confronting the reactionary elements in Congress. This makes all the more logical his overtures to the European Union in which he implored that 'it convince' the parliaments in its member states to reject the Helms-Burton Act. In reply the European Foreign Affairs Commissioner Leon Brittan told Warren Christopher, US Secretary of State, that to adopt the provisions of this bill would 'reactivate our long-standing differences regarding its unilateral and extraterritorial aspects [by having] an immediate impact on EU business interests'.[11]

It is not known if Clinton's efforts bore fruit. It is certain that a few days later, in mid-April, the *New York Times* reported that Canada, France and the UK had undertaken an unprecedented campaign to prevent the bill's approval, arguing that it would place improper pressure on other countries to follow the policies of Washington. For what it was worth, the EU also made more timid statements against it.

INTOLERANCE

In the summer of 1994, faced with the problems caused in the United States by the *balseros* [rafters] (people leaving Cuba aboard anything that would float as a result of the dire economic situation of the time), President Clinton was forced to go back and negotiate with the Cuban government on the question of migration. It was proof that he was aware of the seriousness of the crisis.

Miami Cuban conservatives responded angrily. They interpreted the question of the emigrants as part of a secret plan that Clinton was hatching with Havana. According to this group, there was the possibility that the president was preparing for the partial lifting of the blockade, as had recently occurred with Vietnam. Organisations such as the Cuban American National Foundation and that of the terrorist Orlando Bosch therefore called for a 'great patriotic strike' to include the withdrawal of labour from shops, businesses and factories.[12] They publicly called on the US government to halt the repatriation of *balseros* together with the immediate withdrawal of negotiations with Havana. Two of their demands in particular came as no surprise: 'the acceptance of the preparation of military action against Fidel Castro's government' and a call to revoke 'the agreements with the old Soviet Union made during the Cuban Missile Crisis in 1962 and in which the US undertook not to invade Cuba'.

In response to the strike call, Xiomara Lindner, adviser to Rodolfo Ruíz, president of Bacardí Imports, confirmed that 'we will support any action necessary'.[13] At about the same time, around 1,000 people travelled from Miami to Washington to protest outside the White House, waving placards proclaiming Clinton to be on the side of communism. The recently merged Bacardí-Martini consortium lent a number of buses to transfer the protesters.[14]

'AN EMOTIONAL ACT'

One of those to extort the most benefit from the so-called *balseros* crisis was the Cuban-American José Basulto, a Bay of Pigs mercenary, CIA agent and Contras adviser. Basulto founded the organisation Brothers to the Rescue (*Hermanos al Rescate* – HAR), together with Bill Schuss, another CIA veteran with expertise in infiltration tactics and commando raids.[15] Its ostensible aim was to deliver supplies by air to *balseros* drifting in the Florida Straits. In these efforts Basulto and Schuss relied upon contributions made by the Cuban American National Foundation and American Airlines; Gloria Estefan and her husband Emilio, both members of the Bacardí family;[16] as well as others. For its part, in April 1994 Bacardí Imports sponsored a collection on behalf of Brothers to the Rescue in the Bacardí Gallery in Miami, raising $72,937.[17]

Brothers to the Rescue did save some lives, but behind the scenes another far from altruistic agenda was taking shape. In their US-based light aircraft, Basulto and his associates systematically invaded Cuban airspace as far as the Havana shoreline, dropping thousands of leaflets urging acts of civil disobedience and insurgency.[18] This was to continue until 24 February 1996 when the Revolutionary Air Force shot down two planes.

On 12 March, 'in an act of pure emotion', Clinton ratified the Liberty and Democratic Solidarity with Cuba Act, better known as the Helms-Burton Law.[19] In the assessment of John Kavulich, president of the US-Cuban Economic and Business Council, a grouping of around 100 American companies, the shooting down of the light aircraft 'meant that the Helms-Burton Act was bound to come into force and Clinton could do nothing to stop it. Moreover, he decided to sign it in spite of the revulsion felt by businessmen in my country towards any attempt by politicians to limit their scope.'[20]

TITLES I AND II

For Cuba, the contents and aims of the Helms-Burton Law are just an updated version of what had already been determined for her at the beginning of the nineteenth century. John Quincy Adams, then US Secretary of State, wrote in 1823 that 'it is almost impossible to resist the notion that the annexation of Cuba into our federal republic will be vital for the continuity and integrity of the Union'.

The Helms-Burton Law contains four articles, or titles as they are called. The first two outline what the Cuban nation must do in order to obtain US designation as a democracy and thereby attain the normalisation of diplomatic relations. Without analysing the minutiae, the text is so severe and over-arching that doubtless not even the laws and treaties imposed on African colonies by the European powers have contained such a degree of arrogance and lack of respect for a sovereign nation recognised by almost every other nation in the world.

In summary, the law states that every avenue should be opened up to the so-called internal opposition, which under its provisions receives more aid and finance from Washington than ever before. The Cuban political leadership must be dismantled together with the Communist Party, grassroots organisations and everything else to do with the current system. This would be followed by a 'transition' period to last as long as it would take for the creation of a new kind of state and society to the liking of the US President, as he and he alone may decide if democracy has arrived in Cuba.

Yet the only ultimate and incontrovertible proof of democracy's arrival would be the US President's confirmation to his trustees involved in the 'transition' that all nationalised property belonging to US citizens or companies had been returned or compensated for, including those of Cuban American magnates. A strange way to determine democracy indeed.

TITLES OF DISCORD

In spite of the grave threat to Cuban sovereignty posed by Titles I and II the international furore was to be targeted at Titles III and IV of the Helms-Burton Law.

Article III, in somewhat confused language, warns anyone who:

sells, transfers, distributes, shares out, exchanges, manages or by other means disposes of confiscated property; or purchases, leases, receives, possesses, controls, manages, uses or by other means obtains confiscated property or has an interest in such. Such are participating in commercial activity in which use or other benefit may be derived from confiscated property ...; it is warned that they will, as a result, be declared 'traffickers'.

A description until then reserved for use in international circles for a type of common delinquent activity. As traffickers, English investors, for example, would be hauled before the US. courts by any US businesses or individuals whose property had been 'illegally confiscated'.

In Cuba, in accordance with international convention still in place and signed by the US, property had been confiscated lawfully and nationalised through the legal actions of the state. This even extended to the signing of agreements for compensation by the Cuban government with those overseas companies and individuals affected. The only exception to this was the US. Hermenegildo Altozano, a Spanish lawyer specialising in international investments, maintains:

The government that emerged after the 1959 Revolution was legally constituted, recognised internationally and followed expropriation procedures in accordance with the legislation then extant in Cuba [and prior to the declaration of the revolution as being of a socialist nature]. This is recognised as such by international law, one of the principles of which, *lex rei sitiae*, establishes that it is the law in force within the territory where property is located which determines the rules over the said property. This was recognised as such by the US Supreme Court in 1964 in the case of the Cuban National Bank v Peter F.L. Sabbatino: in applying the doctrine of the Sovereign State Act by virtue of which US courts of law could not pass judgement on the legality or otherwise of expropriations made by a foreign government, in this case that of Cuba: in territory within which said government exercised sovereign jurisdiction [...][21]

In summary the Helms-Burton Law is not only a violation of international convention but even of the US's own laws.

At Helms's insistence the references to the recovery of nationalised property constituted one of the areas of most detailed study for the working party brought together to bring the bill about. It occurred to this group that US legislation permitted those of its citizens who had been subject to torture in another country to bring foreign nationals to trial in the US: a right also held by those with confiscated or nationalised property. In a press conference Dan Fisk, the man heading the working party, was to explain: 'I find it very interesting that we do more to protect marine life than the rights of property claimants ...'[22]

Fisk, Helms and the other proponents of the bill had no qualms whatsoever in asserting that the right of businesses and their wealthy citizens to ownership of property free from the threat of expropriation should be enshrined in the Universal Declaration of Human Rights.

Title IV of the Act bans all 'traffickers' in Cuban properties, in other words company directors, advisers, their relatives and so on, from entering US territory. It takes no account of the fact that many companies investing in Cuba also have businesses in the US. This title is not subject to suspension or negotiation by the president of the United States, unlike Title III, which the president can suspend temporarily as long as the motive is in line with some form of pressure being applied to the Cuban government. This was the first time ever that the Chief of the White House had been stripped by Congress of any of his powers in the field of foreign policy.

NEGOTIATIONS BEHIND THE SCENES

Almost as soon as Clinton had ratified the bill, Jesse Helms was to warn in undiplomatic terms in an article written for *Global Viewpoint* at the end of 1996 and printed in several US and European publications that:

> [...] The threat of legal action remains hanging over the heads of Castro's business friends like a guillotine and sooner or later the guillotine will fall [...] these traffickers should have the decency to sit down, shut up and put a stop to these lies that the US is a bad neighbour or untrustworthy ally. They are the bad neighbours, deserving neither respect nor sympathy.

So it came to pass. Just a few days after the bill passed into law its effects were to be felt. The directors and shareholders of the Italian company Stet, the Mexican company Domos and the Canadian company Sherritt all received a warning from the US government. Each was threatened with the withdrawal of US entry visas if they did not cease 'trafficking' in nationalised property with Cuba. Identical intimidation was subsequently dispatched to the Israeli agricultural company BM, the Spanish tour operator Sol-Meliá and the French drinks concern Pernod-Ricard. By the first anniversary of the Act becoming law the US State Department was holding to ransom nearly 25 companies in 11 countries.

In an attempt to dispel the storm clouds gathering around him towards the end of 1996 Clinton attempted to reach agreement with the European Union, using as an intermediary the Spanish government led by José María Aznar. He did not choose him by chance. The latter had close links with the Miami extreme right, to the extent that he had made use of the Cuban National American Foundation aircraft to tour Miami, Costa Rica and El Salvador during his Spanish election campaign.[23] It was, therefore, no surprise in November 1996 to witness Aznar putting forward a series of proposals to the European Union so blatantly inspired by US policy towards Cuba that the Spanish newspaper *El País* was moved to print the following headline: 'Spain's Proposal to the Fifteen [member states] a carbon copy of US demands to the EU'.

The proposals, known as the Common Position, were approved by the European Commission in record time and without significant changes. The EU therefore fell into step with the designated US policy of political, financial and economic pressure on Cuba to ease the 'road to democracy'. The Common Position makes it clear that a deepening economic involvement by Europe in Cuba is dependent on Cuba making changes to its political and economic system that is, moving towards multi-party democracy and a free market economy. To Cuba's cost the European Union therefore collaborated with Clinton in order to give him the excuse to suspend temporarily the implementation of the provisions of Title III.

In an attempt to salvage some pride, in October 1996 the European Union lodged a claim against the US with the World Trade Organisation (WTO). This was based on the illegality of the Helms-Burton Act in so far as it was an attack upon international free trade regulations, even to the extent of violating those which the US had itself pushed to be approved by international institutions. Faced with this claim, the US responded by stating that if the WTO were to condemn their actions they would resort to a clause in the organisation's constitution which would permit the refusal to accept a decision against it based on the grounds of risk to 'national security'. As the experts acknowledged it was a somewhat ludicrous scenario to imagine that an organisation such as the WTO could endanger the US in such a way. The EU's bravery was to prove short-lived. In April 1997, Leon Brittan, supported by the Council of European Ministers, withdrew the claim completely. At this time and in total secrecy the 29 richest nations in the world were in negotiations with the Organisation for Economic Co-operation and Development (OECD) over what was to be called the Multilateral Investment Agreement (MIA). In all the dealings over the MIA, no arguments were ever raised about the consequences of the Helms-Burton Act. On the contrary, the Act's aims were underpinned and reinforced by the crucial points in the agreement concerning the protection of investments made by this exclusive club of nations in any part of the world; in other words, the outlawing of a state's ability to confiscate and nationalise their property.

THE BIRMINGHAM AGREEMENT

The dispute between the US and the European Union would go on as a result of continuing and sustained investment in Cuba by EU businesses. On 18 May 1998 an agreement was reached to the satisfaction of all parties: the Birmingham Agreement. Within its main points, the European Union, in shameful fashion, accepted the internationalisation of the blockade against Cuba in spite of the fact that the majority of its members had continually rejected it in the United Nations. It officially acknowledges the illegality of the nationalisation of US-owned property in Cuba subject to EU 'supervision' of the work of the Overseas Claims Procedure Group in Washington.

It is worth highlighting that the European Union finds fault only now with these expropriations and nationalisations. At the time they were made, European countries had come to agreement with Havana over compensation and had been quite content to do so. This is just as illogical as the decision to go ahead with the agreement without consulting the other party directly implicated: Cuba herself.

Secretary of State Madeleine Albright sent a memo to Jesse Helms on 3 August 1998 in which she commented on the success of her government in securing the Birmingham Agreement and in the course of which she states:

> [...] the European Union has finally accepted the illegality of the expropriation of US property. This recognition forms an integral part of the Agreement. This is an extraordinary vindication for the principles which form the basis for the Act of Democratic Solidarity and Liberty for Cuba. The Agreement constitutes another filter designed to prevent the provision of any type of aid or financial assistance to investment in potentially illegally seized property. Once we inform the EU of the existence of these provisions, as already made in the case of Cuba, it will implement this filter and must maintain close links with ourselves [...] The US-EU Agreement will strengthen the protection afforded to all those US citizens from whom property has been illegally expropriated, including those claims made by naturalised Cuban Americans [...] if the EU does not comply with its obligations the Act of Liberty will continue to be a powerful weapon in achieving our political aims. You have my assurance that, in the case where the Agreement were not upheld, I would not hesitate to lift the suspension of Title IV [...] It is vital that we do not waste this unique and historical opportunity to achieve the aims of the Act of Liberty and establish wider reaching and new property protection rights for all US citizens in Cuba and the rest of the world [...]

11 'The Bacardí Claims Act'

A WHISPER TAKES SHAPE

> In February the Miami office of the legal firm Kelley and Warren (sic) issued a press release lauding the involvement of one of its lawyers, Ignacio Sánchez, in the 'editing and revision' of the Helms-Burton Bill [...][1]

This press release could be viewed as routine given the prevailing attitude in a place like Miami where making a name for oneself ranks above any sense of professional ethics. However, in this instance this was not the case. It was the first confirmation of a rumour that for several days had done the rounds of various corridors and offices in Washington, Miami and New York. This was just hours after Jesse Helms had presented his bill in public and as Clinton began to receive the first worried responses from both home and abroad.

Faced with a barrage of criticisms and questions from all sections of the media and political organisations and figures and whilst attempting to play down the importance of the matter, Sánchez felt obliged to state that the release had been an exaggeration on the part of the firm's publicity agent.[2]

A VERY DIFFERENT LUNCH

On Monday 17 April 1995 and with his bill recently passed by the House of Representatives Sub-Committee on Western Hemisphere Affairs, Helms travelled to Miami as the guest of the Cuban

American National Foundation. While there he pursued various aims including canvassing for support for his bill and seeking financial assistance. A few lines taken from a local newspaper illustrate what happened during the most crucial act during his stay:

> [...] We went through into the dining room where lunch was taken in an atmosphere of true patriotism and which was attended by many of the most representative and distinguished Cuban exile groups [...] Then Pepe Hernández, President of the Cuban American National Foundation, gave a speech of real restraint yet heartfelt patriotism which was heard with rapt attention.
>
> Next up to speak was [...] Rodolfo A Ruíz, president of Bacardí Imports, who eloquently addressed the audience expressing the feelings of all those present that it was imperative to see a Free Cuba [...]
>
> Senator Helms stepped on to the platform to outline his thoughts and reiterate the stance he had maintained since first entering the Senate in 1972 and ever since: that he had always been a staunch defender of democracy for Cuba and a dedicated fighter on behalf of the freedom of all peoples, on this occasion by presenting a Bill that would worsen the economy for the oppressive Havana regime [...][3]

Such an event might appear of little or no significance to the unprepared reader. However, it confirms yet again the close relationship between Bacardí shareholders and the Cuban American National Foundation. Nonetheless the press release by the agency Kelley Drye & Warren did contain an apparently trivial item which is illuminating and was reported by several US news sources. The *Baltimore Sun*, in a lengthy article on 22 May 1995, revealed that, 'Bacardí executives, in fact, joined Jorge Mas Canosa, who heads the Cuban-American National Foundation, a high-powered conservative lobbying organisation, in sponsoring a fund-raising lunch for Mr Helms in Miami in April which grossed more than $75,000.' The lunch provoked so much distrust regarding its motives that as late as 15 July the *Miami Herald* reported:

> In April the head of the Bacardí's Miami-based subsidiary, Rodolfo Ruíz, co-hosted a $500-a-plate fund-raiser for Helms in Miami. The host of the event, which netted an estimated

$75,000 for Helms, was the Cuban American National Foundation
[...]

But why waste so much ink on a press release for a dinner for a
senator? The bill's supporters maintained that it would accelerate
the fall of Castro and 'the advent of a new democratic era' in Cuba,
whereas its detractors were convinced otherwise. The Miami
newspaper *El Nuevo Herald* reported on 15 July:

> The bill contains measures that will benefit businesses such as
> Bacardí and the Fanjul family of sugar magnates. This is normal
> given the tradition that exists in the US of lobbying in Congress
> on behalf of private interests: in this case, however, criticisms
> are raised due to its openly stated political aims [...][4]

This is at the core of the controversy and criticism. Little wonder
then, as acknowledged in the same article in the *Miami Herald*,
that 'in Congressional circles' the proposals put forward by Helms
and Burton were labelled the 'Bacardí Bill'. Still others, such as
the ex-chief of the United States Special Interests Section in Havana,
Wayne Smith, preferred to call it the 'Bacardí Claims Act'.

It fell upon Juan Prado, company shareholder and adviser to
the head of the board of directors of Bacardí in Miami, to come
out and try to untangle the mess: 'He said the Foundation had
asked for help in filling tables at the event, and Bacardí responded
positively. "We as a company couldn't do anything," he said, "but
we as individual persons wanted to help [...]".'[5] This statement
was not widely believed. Any remaining credibility was shattered
a little later when Prado himself admitted: 'Bacardí would be a
prime beneficiary if the Helms bill became law.'[6]

AN ABSURD CALCULATION

'Although the company's headquarters are in Bermuda,' commented
a press statement, 'its US subsidiaries or any one of the around
500 family members who have become citizens of our country
could benefit from this Act and lodge claims in the courts.'[7]

According to the experts it is apparent that one of the craziest
aspects of Helms-Burton is the inclusion of powerful Cuban-
American magnates among those demanding the return of
nationalised property. To grant these individuals the opportunity

to take to court any foreign citizen who had trafficked in 'their' property is absurd given international law and customs. The Under-Secretary of State for Political Affairs, Peter Tarnoff, testified before Congress:

> When a state expropriates property within its own borders belonging to its own nationals, the United States has no recognised basis under international claims law for asserting a connection to the state's action [...] That the national in question may subsequently become, or transfer the claim to the property to, a US citizen does not alter this fact.[8]

Another point concerns the class-based bias in the bill as shown by its favouring an exclusive club of Cuban-Americans: powerful landowners, sugar plantation owners and refiners, farmers and distillers – such as Bacardí – the millionaire class at the time of the revolution. The law, according to a Miami lawyer quoted by the *Miami Herald*, required the Cuban-American claimant to demonstrate 'that the property was worth a minimum of $50,000 at the time of confiscation'. Given this condition, the lawyer went on, 'If there are 100 claims I reckon that's going to be a lot.'[9]

Clinton and the State Department were not the only ones worried about Title III being put into effect. The Joint Corporate Committee on Cuban Claims, an organisation of US companies that had lost property in Cuba, also opposed the Helms-Burton Act. Among the 30 members of this group are large companies such as Chase Manhattan Bank, Coca-Cola and ITT; claims from the group add up to more than $1 billion before interest.

In theory all 5,911 of the original US claimants stood to benefit from the new legislation. Their disagreement was centred on the unknown number of Cuban-Americans who would end up presenting claims and obtaining a hearing in conflict with their own claims and which will make less likely the possibility of a separate agreement with Havana.[10] Furthermore, any such agreement is rendered impossible as long as Fidel and Raúl Castro remain in the government as the Helms-Burton Law forbids it.

THE EARLIEST PROOF

Here are the words of Álvaro Vargas Llosa, a person with first-hand information:

It would not be accurate to say that the exiles of the Foundation were behind the Act; the truth is they were its vanguard [...] [...] Bacardí, for example. Although not playing a critical role they were there at the birth. Like any company these days they tend to try to avoid public controversy. The Cuban family company tiptoed into its involvement in the running of Cuban exile politics [...] Just handy for anyone the slightest bit malicious would be the straightforward expedient of accusing Bacardí executives of wanting to promote the recovery of their assets in Cuba and the removal from the scene of Pernod-Ricard, the French company responsible for the worldwide distribution of Cuban rum and which coveted the North American market, by using the Machiavellian means of the Act. These first accusations caused Bacardí's bosses to beat a hasty retreat from the limelight. From the shadows, however, its lawyers, allies and adopted sons continued to lend a hand in the legal, political and financial arenas to the anti-Castro coalition dedicated to cutting off Fidel Castro's life support system of foreign investments which had enabled him to survive the drying up of the Soviet stream [...] Although Bacardí's efforts on behalf of the Act could have been stronger given the company's resources, their arrival on the field of play was one notable new facet, among others, *in the amazing story of a legislative event which was to lead to an economic conflict between the mayor (sic) Western powers from March 1996* [...][11] (author's italics)

MORE PROOF

According to none other than Dan Fisk, assistant to Helms, one of the first final drafts of the bill to come out of Helms's office went straight to the Cuban American National Foundation's Washington office. The CANF apparently had little directly to do with the drawing up of the bill but was nevertheless a sensational lobbying machine on its behalf: 'No one lobbied as much, as systematically, or with as much financial clout as CANF', claimed the lawyer Nicolas Gutiérrez.[12]

As has been shown, the legislators pushing for and signing the bill had links with both Bacardí and the CANF thanks to financial contributions to their election campaign funds. It is almost impossible to expect that every single lawyer working with Dan Fisk on the editing, correcting and fine detail of this legislation was or is totally unconnected with the Bacardí empire in any way.[13]

The relationship between these lawyers, their practices and Bacardí may appear to be a complex spider's web, but in reality it is much less complicated than that. It is just another part of the interweaving, intrigues and connections to be found throughout this book (see Appendix I).

The least implicated among the Bacardí empire is Nicolas Gutiérrez, a University of Georgetown graduate, 'who made suggestions while the Helms-Burton Bill was being drawn up and was one of its most ardent supporters'.[14] The son of a sugar magnate in pre-revolutionary Cuba, he is currently secretary of the National Association of Cuban Sugar Refinery Owners, based in Miami, a member of the paramilitary Cuban American Military Council and an associate of the Adorno and Zeder legal practice whose clients include several Cuban millionaires with nationalised property, such as the Fanjul family sugar magnates who were once Cuban-based and are now located in the Dominican Republic and the US.

Gutiérrez's logic regarding Helms-Burton is straightforward: 'The crux of this Act is not whether damages can be claimed or not, but to create enough uncertainty for investors to think twice before going to Cuba. The aim is to get rid of Fidel Castro.'[15]

There is a connection between Gutiérrez, Bacardí and even the CANF: the international grouping Adorno and Zeder. Henry Adorno and Raúl Cantero are part of this legal practice and were also lawyers for the man who built the Bacardí empire: José Pepín Bosch. Cantero continues to work for Bacardí. Adorno has been a director and lawyer for the Foundation and in addition not just legal representative for the Mas Canosa family but also vice-chairman of his principal company, Mastec.

AND YET MORE PROOF

Ignacio Sánchez, Miami lawyer and member of the American Bar Association's Cuban Property Rights Task Force, testified to and fiercely supported the Senate's approval of the Helms-Burton Law. When his agency Kelley Drye & Warren released the press communiqué in which he was congratulated for his important contributions to the Act and his relations with Bacardí, he emphasised that he 'helped Helms's aides draft the section of the bill relating to property claims'.[16] Without denying that Bacardí stood to be one of the main beneficiaries were the bill to be passed, he maintained that the multinational 'had not paid him for regular consultations made by members of Helms's team'.[17] He stated that his advice was given as a member of a legal practice and not as part of Bacardí. Strange, then, that Kelley Drye & Warren represent Bacardí in New York and that Sánchez is a director of the Cuban American National Foundation. Another member of the legal profession to work for Helms and his bill was Brice Clagett of the Washington legal firm Covington and Burling who represent several US companies with nationalised property in Cuba. This group, which lobbies on behalf of Bacardí in the capital, is of crucial importance. For many years and until very recently the group had among its members a unique Bacardí figure: George Chip Reid.

Chip, one time legal consultant to the Republican Party, has possibly been Bacardí's closest and most valued adviser to the extent that he was crucial in the acquisition of Martini & Rossi, the world famous Italian company. Reid is no longer with the firm simply because in 1997 he moved to Miami to occupy the chair of board of directors of Bacardí USA Inc., leapfrogging from there to Bermuda as chairman of the board of directors of the empire, although under the tutelage of Cutillas. Chip, US citizen through and through, was the first non-Bacardí family member to occupy this position.

Robert Freer Jr, associate of the firm Freer and McGarry, also served as an adviser during the drafting of the bill. Freer is executive secretary of the US-Cuba Business Council, the private body closest to the Helms and Burton team.[18] Also on the council executive is Juan Prado, an important Bacardí shareholder and director. Moreover, the chairman of the council during the time that the Helms-Burton Bill was being drafted and subsequently passed was the principal Bacardí boss, Manuel J. Cutillas.

The president of the Business Council's management team is the Cuban-American Otto Reich, who 'was one of those who, on Bacardí's behalf, wove part of the Helms-Burton web'.[19] Reich has been more helpful than any other diplomat on behalf of the Cuban American National Foundation and in particular the Bacardí multinational. He has a curriculum vitae which stretches from his time as US army officer in the Panama Canal Zone to ambassador. In addition one must not forget his involvement in the running of the Center for a Free Cuba along with Jeanne Kirkpatrick, Luis

Aguilar León, William Doherty and the main chief of Bacardí, Manuel J. Cutillas, who is also president of the Council of Administration.[20] Speaking of the Center for a Free Cuba, it has to be highlighted that together with the CANF this was one of the organisations most active in applying pressure and manipulating and investing huge amounts of money in its attempts to gain the granting of political asylum in the US to the child Elián González against the wishes of his father and international law, using him as a weapon against the Cuban government. However, after detaining him for seven months the US authorities allowed the return of the child to his home country. In the meantime, his father had refused an offer of $2 million from the Cuban-American extreme right to claim political asylum together with his family. This was a bitter blow to this powerful political faction.

As further evidence of Reich's fundamental links with Bacardí we can cite his directorship on the board of affairs of the Brock Consultancy Group. The diplomat has been a director of the Brock Group, a firm which lobbies in the US on behalf of the German Ministry of Trade and British American Tobacco. It represents the Bacardí empire in similar fashion in Washington, Bermuda and the Bahamas. According to declassified Federal documents Brock received more than $110,000 from Bacardí during the six most decisive months in the passage of the Helms-Burton Bill.[21] Not to mention the fact that Reich was amongst the first to testify before the US Congress in favour of the bill on 30 June 1995 in his capacity as chairman of the Business Council.

BACARDÍ, THOUGH NOT US ...

As acknowledged by a highly placed executive within the multinational, Bacardí is a 'stateless company', with offices in Bermuda.[22] In spite of this, using its economic weight together with contacts in influential political circles it practically wrote its own United States legislation, accommodating its wishes into the Act in the process. The Helms-Burton Law, as it has become known, is not just an attack on Cuban sovereignty and the survival of its citizens. It also contributes to the madness caused by the dangerous sliding of the capitalist economic system when it undergoes the trauma of wanting to sweep away even the tiniest of barriers to its global advance.

12 Market 'Wars'

SUBTLE THREATS

In the summer of 1993 there was a constant rumour that the Cuban government was negotiating an agreement with a foreign company for the international marketing of Havana Club, its most well-known brand of rum. This set the alarm bells ringing in the Bacardí multinational which had just acquired Martini & Rossi.

For Manuel J. Cutillas and his fellow shareholders the situation was worrying. Firstly, a real competitor could threaten their near monopoly in the rum market. Secondly, it would be 'leeching' from the property they once owned and thereby providing the suffocating Cuban economy with some much needed oxygen. Thirdly, it flew in the face of the Torricelli-Graham Act that they had done so much to support.

Consequently Cutillas began to send letters to associations and to the heads of corporations involved with the production and distribution of spirits in which a definite threatening tone can be detected. One in particular was dispatched from Nassau to Robert Maxwell, chairman of the United States' National Association of Drinks Importers. Dated 28 October 1993, its most salient paragraphs state:

[...] The properties confiscated from Bacardí included the Bacardí distillery and corporate office building in Santiago de Cuba, another corporate office building in Havana, three Hatuey breweries and the Hatuey trademark. By this means we seek your understanding of Bacardí's position and your co-operation in promoting an industry-wide consensus in favour of the approach described below.

It is Bacardí's position, supported by expert legal advice, that its confiscated assets continue to be its lawful property, and that no one who accepts a purported conveyance of any such property from the Castro regime will acquire good title under either Cuban or international law. Once the rule of law and representative government are restored in Cuba, Bacardí intends to take every appropriate step both to recover its properties and also to seek appropriate compensation from those who have acquired from the present regime, exploited and misused those properties during the period when Bacardí was deprived of their possession.

Bacardí confidently expects that under a future democratic government traditional constitutional guarantees will be restored and unlawful conveyances by the Castro regime will not be recognised by the courts as passing good title, implement Bacardí's right to recover damages from anyone who has occupied and exploited Bacardí's properties at any time during the Castro regime. Bacardí fully intends to claim all such damages that may be recoverable, including rent, unjust enrichment from any profits that may have been realised, damages from unlawful use of trademarks or patents, deterioration of physical facilities and environmental harm, plus interest and possibly punitive damages [...]

Finally, potential investors should be aware that Bacardí has taken successful legal action in the past against the current government of Cuba. These legal actions [...] have spanned decades since the Castro government first confiscated the Bacardí properties in Cuba [...] While we are prepared to take those kinds of action in the future to recover our property, we sincerely hope that will not be necessary.

We take this opportunity to express our appreciation for any co-operation which you may be able to extend to our company's efforts and request that you distribute this letter to your member companies.

A COINCIDENTAL WARNING

By chance, a few months earlier, several extremist organisations, including the Cuban American National Foundation, had sent an 'open letter' to a large number of businesses and industries in Europe and Latin America. The theme was almost identical:

We, the undersigned, have every intention of taking part in the creation of a new republic in a Cuba without Castro [...] We maintain that any investment made in Cuba in present circumstances will not warrant consideration by the laws on private property to be formulated by a future Cuban government [...] We believe that it is imperative that the international investment community is aware of our intentions, and that those thinking of investing in Cuba take into account fully the political implications of such actions and the risks they may run [...]

THE OBJECT OF FEAR: PERNOD-RICARD

Cutillas wasn't wrong in feeling both worried and threatened in 1993. That year, the Cuban company Havana Rum and Liquors (HRL) and the French plc Pernod-Ricard signed a joint-venture agreement (50 per cent of the capital and equally shared risks) to market Havana Club rum. The Cuban economy, almost shipwrecked, now had the important lifeline of foreign investment in order to obtain the foreign currency necessary to ensure arrival in safe waters.

As genuine Cuban rum and with the marketing expertise of the French multinational, Havana Club shot up the sales list as soon as it was launched in 1994, thereby taking a market share from Bacardí. Cutillas himself acknowledged in *El Nuevo Herald* in March 1996 that 'trade has stood still for the last two or three years'.

Before 1994 Bacardí had no rival worthy of the name. Cuba had concentrated nearly all its rum distribution in the East European socialist bloc. The breach being opened up by Cuban rum had to be seen to be believed. In 1998, Havana Club was producing 1 million cases a year for the first time and was one of the three fastest-growing brands in the world. It has continued to be so since then.[1]

Pernod-Ricard ran the risk of a showdown with both Bacardí and US law, not because of any charitable feelings or a desire to express solidarity with the Cuban revolution but because they were aware that it made good business sense.

Bacardí didn't take long to conclude that the success of Havana Club was in large part due to its 100 per cent Cuban origins. Knowing full well that to do so would fool the consumer and trample over international convention, it wholeheartedly 'reinvented' itself as Cuban. Bacardí shifted from hating Cuba (from 1960) and from prohibiting any mention of Cuba in its advertising to seeing itself as more Cuban than a cigar (from 1994 onwards). An unimaginable 360-degree shift. Even George Chip Reid, who was to be chairman of the empire until March 2000, dared to proclaim, 'We are proud of our Cuban heritage.'[2] The historical irony was that just as Bacardí was coming to accept its 'heritage' it was being headed by a US citizen who had never set foot on Cuban soil.

DECEITFUL PROPAGANDA

Facundo Bacardí-Mazó had already said at the end of the nineteenth century that:

Historically there really has never been nor shall there ever be in any country anywhere a rum like ours. Not even anything remotely like it. Those that make it elsewhere do not have at their disposal the best raw materials there are, namely the syrup of Cuban sugar cane.[3]

Since 1994 Bacardí have attributed several phrases to Don Facundo in their advertising campaign. The above quote, however, remains locked in the dustiest corner of the rum empire's memory banks. It does not feature in their tightly controlled affirmation of 'Cubanism', a 'Cubanism' which in the 1940s was called into question by the investigator Jacinto Torras and has remained so ever since (see Chapter 2).

Never in the history of advertising can there have been a campaign in which there featured so many references to a product's origin without one single mention of the fact that the product in question was made anywhere other than in its claimed country of origin; in Bacardí's case not even the label, nor the bottle itself, still less one single drop of the liquor. Nothing. In all the furore of the Bacardí advertising campaign the words 'Cuba' and 'Santiago de Cuba' are essential. These have helped convince many consumers that they were paying for a Cuban rum, a manoeuvre that the

World Organisation for Intellectual Property Rights (WOIPR) has described as 'contrary to honest use'.[4] Ever since the Bacardí shareholders left the island (not forgetting that the most valuable of all their assets, their trademark, had been carried off to the Bahamas years before the triumph of the Revolution), Bacardí labels have unreservedly claimed that this was a product manufactured in Puerto Rico. Some time later, some labels would say that the liquor was from the Bahamas. Although the syrup could have come from cane grown anywhere in the Caribbean, Brazil, Mexico or Florida (and noting that it is the cane that gives rum its quality and distinct 'personality'), at least one was given a clue as to where the mixture was distilled. These references were to all but disappear in the mid-1990s.

From 1998 the distinctive bat logo was joined by the phrase 'company founded in Santiago de Cuba in 1862', although 'Estd. Cuba 1862' has become more commonplace. On some labels 'Product of Bahamas' can be found, although on the great majority of these there is no indication whatsoever as to which country it is produced in. In Spain, for example, the labels simply read 'Bottled by authority and to the specifications of Bacardí and Company Limited', but in most cases they just say 'Imported and distributed by ...'. In no instance is it specified where it has been imported from and nothing at all is said about where it is distilled.

'CUBA LIBRE'

In a victory for the Spanish state's Association of Advertising Users (AUC), in mid-December 1999, a legal ruling prevented Bacardí from continuing to advertise 'Cuba Libre' in cans on television. The decision concluded that the campaign constituted indirect publicity for Bacardí rum which, with an alcohol content exceeding 20 per cent by volume, rendered such advertising illegal in that country. According to the AUC press release the ruling stated that this represented a form of unfair competition with other spirit-based drinks with a high alcohol content. Furthermore, the release went on saying that the advert in question could 'mislead the viewer as to the true nature of the product' because it had much in common with adverts for Bacardí rum and their many shots of the Caribbean, scenes that the viewer could interpret as being of Cuba.

It is also important to mention that it was only in 1998 that Bacardí called the blend 'Cuba Libre'. Since 1966, when it had joined forces with Coca-Cola to produce the cocktail, it had simply called it 'Rum and Coke' or 'Bacardí and Coke'.[5]

If one wishes to discover the true origin of this concoction the version offered by Bacardí is not satisfactory in spite of company assurances that it was the inventor of the drink in 1898. This account is constantly changing, even within the same country. Sometimes it claims to have started in Santiago de Cuba, on other occasions in Havana. But there is a thread of consistency: it is always a US serviceman (sometimes an officer, sometimes a rating) who mixes the ingredients to drink a toast to a 'Free Cuba' (sometimes with a Cuban, sometimes alone). A historical irony, given that it was the same army which, at its own instigation, became involved in the War of Independence declared by Cuban patriots to rid themselves of the Spanish, and that, once the troops from the Iberian Peninsula had been got rid of, the gringos who raised a toast to a 'Free Cuba' stayed and converted the country into a pseudo-colony.

13 More Than a Rum 'War'

UNFAIR COMPETITION?

Perhaps as a result of Havana Club's commercial success and the start of what may be regarded as the contemporary rum 'war' in mid-1996, Bacardí began the distribution and sale of a rum produced in the Bahamas and called 'Havana Club' in the United States. The label showed the Malecón seafront in the Cuban capital along with the slogan 'Discover the flavour of old Havana'. Bacardí was only able to succeed in importing 96 cases when the Havana Club Holding group, a consortium created by the Cuban and French companies, had a claim substantiated for fraud, theft of brand name and consumer deception. The empire was using a brand name that had never belonged to it; moreover, it was a name which since 1974 had been registered in the United States to a Cuban company following the abandonment of its registration by the original holder.

It should be recalled that in 1995 there was an expectation, albeit ill-founded, that President Clinton was about, at least partially, to lift the trade blockade against Cuba. For those who believed this, it was a near certainty that the reintroduction of Cuban rum would be allowed; and were this the case the Bacardí multinational's kingdom would be in a fix given that it enjoyed a 50 per cent share of the US market. This led to its wholehearted support, dictated by a combination of commercial greed and the worry caused by foreseeing Cuba once again in the United States' embrace, for the Helms-Burton Act.

Doubtless the launch of these counterfeit bottles surprised more than a few people. Such an act of piracy was not to be expected from such a prestigious brand, still less so when one considers it was against the interests of another powerful drinks multinational like Pernod-Ricard.

In July 1994, Bacardí-Martini delivered a request to the US Patent and Trademark Office for six brand names, all containing the word Havana: 'Little Havana', 'Old Havana', 'Havana Select', 'Havana Clipper', 'Havana Classical' and 'Havana Primo'. Four years were to pass before the office would decide that it would only accept the registration of the first of these, as the others would confuse the consumer who might think that he or she was paying for a product 'made in Cuba'. In September 1994 Galleon, a Bacardí subsidiary in the Bahamas, tried to register the trademark 'Havana Club' in the United States. The request was thrown out. However, this did not make the multinational lose heart.

THE OWNER CANNOT CHOOSE

Bacardí-Martini's assault on the Franco-Cuban consortium was becoming more intense. In the first quarter of 1996 and soon after the Helms-Burton Act had been ratified by Clinton, Bacardí informed the US authorities that Pernod-Ricard was using its old property in Cuba. This action had a sole aim: to accuse the French company of trafficking in confiscated property.

The Franco-Cuban company maintains that Pernod-Ricard is not trafficking in confiscated property. It asserts that the two installations where the rum is distilled were constructed after the Revolution on land which never belonged to Bacardí. However, Bacardí-Martini insists on refusing any excuses and in doing so depends on the Helms-Burton Act. Havana Club rum is produced using nationalised property. This is completely false according to the Cubans and French and can be refuted instantly.

In the knowledge that the Cuban company would have to renew ownership of the brand in 1996, Bacardí-Martini began putting pressure on the responsible authorities to ensure that it would be revoked. It did not succeed and Havana Club once again, for a 20-year period, received the protection afforded by US law and international conventions. There was one further detail: the brand's ownership was now in the hands of the Franco-Cuban consortium Havana Club Holding, a severe blow to the multinational.

However, Bacardí did not lose any time. While it continued applying pressure on the US Copyright Office, at the same time it approached the US Treasury, whose responsibility it was to decide whether or not any decision was in breach of the blockade against Cuba. In its demand, Bacardí-Martini claimed that the Cuban company had breached the blockade by transferring the brand name to its French counterpart. The office charged with deciding this within the US Treasury itself, OFAC, accepted its arguments. In April 1997, a federal judge, basing his decision on that of OFAC and other claims made by Bacardí-Martini, ordered that the licence be withdrawn from the Franco-Cuban consortium. A case where the owner cannot decide the destiny of his own property.

HE WHO LIVES BY THE NEWS ...

At the same time, several news sources around the world launched a series of reports on alleged corruption at the highest level in Cuba. These were based on an item in *Forbes* magazine, the publication aimed at investors and whose proprietor has been closely linked to the Republican Party and the Cuban American National Foundation.[1] The reports asserted that Fidel Castro was 'one of the richest men in the world' thanks to funds appropriated from the state. Simultaneously, a widely reported investigation undertaken by two Cuban Americans reached the same conclusion as *Forbes*.

Days later, on 18 August 1997, the Spanish news agency EFE published a report which went almost unnoticed. The cable stated that these 'financial irregularities committed by the Cuban government', including Castro's supposed thousands, had come to light 'following an investigation made by the Bacardí company during its case against Pernod-Ricard [...]'

THE RETURN OF BACARDÍ'S LEGISLATORS

In July 1997, nearly all the Congressmen and women who, together with Helms and Burton, had pressed for the Act sent a letter to the Secretary for the Treasury, Robert Rubin. In it can clearly be seen the aim of defending the interests of Bacardí-Martini:

We have recently become aware of the decision of your office to revoke a previously granted licence which authorised the transfer for a significant sum by the Cuban government of a trade mark registered with the US Patent and Trademark Office. We refer to the brand Havana Club. We understand that the licence was granted initially due to the misrepresentation by representatives of the Cuban government of the scope and the nature of this transaction to your office.

As you are fully aware, since the commencement of the embargo and through the promulgation of the 1992 Cuban Democracy Act and more recently the Solidarity with Liberty and Democracy Act, it has been the policy of the United States as followed by nine US Presidents with the bipartisan support of Congress to achieve democratic changes in Cuba by applying economic pressure on Castro and depriving him of freely convertible currency. President Clinton has assiduously worked to extend this policy and has made progress in achieving the support of our allies in these efforts.

We understand that as a result of the decision taken on 17 April by OFAC the French government has protested to our State Department. This protest alone should justify OFAC's decision, given that it is highly improbable that the French government would take such an active role had its citizens not paid a significant sum to the government of Cuba for rights to the trade mark in the US ...

[...] Were any other legal move to be undertaken by the Cuban government or its business associates seeking the approval of this legal transaction, we strongly recommend that OFAC continue to apply the principles of our policy towards Cuba and reject any request contrary to this policy [...]

Signed: Jesse Helms, Dan Burton, Robert Torricelli, Robert Menéndez, Ileana Ros-Lehtinen, Robert Graham, Benjamín Gilman, Peter Deutsch.

BACARDÍ 'DISCOVERS' THE ARECHABALAS

Bacardí-Martini's efforts have fundamentally been aimed at wresting the Havana Club brand from its owners. To achieve this end any means have been justified. They therefore sought and effortlessly found the Arechabalas, the descendants of Basque emigrants who at the end of the nineteenth century had produced Havana Club rum in Cuba.

Back then, the Arechabalas' company registered the brand name in five countries. However, four years prior to the Revolution's triumph they did not re-register the brand in Spain or the Dominican Republic. As a result the name passed into what is known as the public domain. This meant that any producer had the right to take the name, register it and begin to produce a rum called Havana Club. The company was bankrupt as a result of its failure to stand up to its competitors, the main one, ironically, being Bacardí.

In 1960, at a virtual standstill due to a wage dispute with its workers caused by the near bankruptcy, the state intervened and nationalised the company. Subsequently, the Arechabalas left Cuba never to return to business with the Havana Club brand. In 1973, when it was time to renew the licence for the Havana Club name, they did not do so in spite of a minimum of red tape and some $ 25 in cost. Moreover, they could even have written an 'affidavit of non-use', to the effect that the brand would have been retained without the requirement to use it.

Given that the name was in the public domain, in 1974 the Cuban company Cubaexport requested the licence for its use and was granted it two years later 'without any legal opposition in respect of this'.[2] The new owner had already succeeded in obtaining the right to use the name in 80 countries (since 1966 in Spain) with no legal claims made against it in any instance.

Yet in 1997 the Arechabala family, most of whom were by now resident in Spain, came to an agreement with Bacardí by which a company was established in Liechtenstein, the favourite European tax haven. From that moment, Bacardí-Martini began to talk of having rights to the brand name as a result of their acquisition from the supposed owners. From this emerged another legal minefield for the Franco-Cuban corporation.

The Arechabalas, aided and abetted by Bacardí-Martini, then decided to take back a brand name which, according to all international agreements and conventions, they had completely abandoned years before. Here one can pose the famous conundrum: who is the father? The man who sired the child only to desert it or the man who reared it? What is certain is that since 1997, the Arechabalas have insisted that Havana Club 'is the property of our family'.[3]

When the question was asked as to why they had never previously attempted to regain the brand name Bacardí-Martini they answered that 'they never had any means to undertake the legal struggle such as that they were now initiating through the lawyers Gómez,

Acebo and Pombo and it could only be undertaken once the family had signed up to an alliance with the Bacardí group'.[4]

This legal dispute in Spain, which appears set to continue elsewhere, would not have been necessary if a few years earlier there had been enough interest in the brand name to pay a few dollars to re-register it.

DYNAMITING THE FACTORY

At the beginning of 1992, the EFE, AFP and Notimex press agencies issued a global release from Miami which went unnoticed by the world's news services. The cables stated that the Cuban Security Services had captured three men who had clandestinely entered the Matanzas Province. They were well equipped with arms and explosives. The agencies were in agreement that one of the tasks that these three people were due to undertake in Cuba was an attack on the old Arechabala drinks factory. At exactly the same time, the Miami extremist groups, led by the Cuban American National Foundation, were reiterating in their press releases that this was one of the companies subject to the Cuban government's negotiations with those parties interested in Havana Club.

What were the aims of this military objective? It is not known. It is certain that these three men declared themselves to be members of the Comandos L faction. In the 1970s this was one of the groups that acted in close collaboration with RECE, the Cuban Representation in Exile, the paramilitary group created by the CIA and the Bacardí magnate, José Pepín Bosch.

Congresswoman Ileana Ros-Lehtinen, one of those closest to Bacardí's political interests and those of the Cuban American National Foundation, took charge of defending them. She requested the help of many public figures to beg Havana for the release of the captives.

BACARDÍ AND THE UNITED STATES AGAINST THE AGREEMENTS

In July 1999, the European Union lodged a claim against the United States at the World Trade Organisation (WTO) in support of the French company Pernod-Ricard and thereby also supporting the Cuban company. Their action argues that the United States 'is in violation of their agreements on Trade Related Aspects of Intellectual

Property (TRIPs)'. Prior to this, the European Union had also protested to Washington that it had failed to keep its part of the Birmingham Agreement of May 1998 that extraterritorial laws were not to be applied, in particular those contained in the Helms-Burton Act (see Chapter 10).

Once again, Europe had had the door slammed in its face after believing the siren calls that the United States had offered as an appeasement to its protests. Once again Cuba was in the thick of it.

The claim lodged by the European Union with the World Trade Organisation went much further than the defence of a French company's business dealings in Cuban rum. In addition to Helms-Burton, Bacardí-Martini had succeeded in securing the passing of new legislation 100 per cent in favour of its interests and which could quickly have adverse effects on other European businesses.

SECTION 211: BY BACARDÍ FOR BACARDÍ

In April 1999 a New York federal court dismissed the claim lodged by Havana Club Holding in 1996 against Bacardí. According to the judge there was no fraud nor consumer deception caused by Bacardí's distribution of 96 cases of a rum called Havana Club produced in the Bahamas.

The decision was based on Section 211, an amendment which came into effect on 21 October 1998, two years after the case had begun and 24 years after Cubaexport had registered the trademark in the United States. Section 211, another nod in the direction of the Helms-Burton Act, was the cause of the spilt milk in the European Union which had led to the claim against the United States with the World Trade Organisation.

Consisting of a dozen lines, it was included in the 1998 Omnibus Appropriations Act containing more than 4,000 pages. It was approved by Congress as a result of a process of expediency which allows the last-minute introduction of various amendments as the great majority of legislators are engaged in the House Senate Conference. Within a few days of its approval it came to light that it was only the politicians with links to Bacardí-Martini who knew its content as there had been no time for others to scrutinise it.

The first sentences of Section 211 declare that the United States courts have no right to recognise the tenure of a trademark or patent by any foreign company which has any connections whatsoever with the property of any US citizen that has been nationalised without compensation by the Cuban revolutionary government. It goes on to outlaw retrospectively the right within the United States for others to own trademarks which had once belonged to Cubans prior to their exile. This includes trademarks that have been relinquished voluntarily or that have passed into the public domain. Only the owner of the confiscated property or their legally recognised heir can consent to their use (this was the 'treaty' made between Bacardí-Martini and the Arechabalas).

Furthermore, it does not allow the United States courts to pronounce unconditionally in cases such as that presented in the late 1990s by Havana Club Holding against Bacardí-Martini and the Arechabalas regarding ownership of the Havana Club trademark. Section 211 denies the judges any professional freedom in these matters.

According to the Cuban government, the amendment 'unjustifiably blocks access to protection within the United States of rights which legitimately correspond to it [...] It deprives any Cuban or Cuban company, or any person acting on behalf of the Cuban authorities of the benefits derived from international conventions and multilateral or bilateral treaties [...]'[5] Such is the case with Havana Club Holding, as it affects in particular the application of the Treaty on Trade Related Aspects of Intellectual Property (TRIPs) to Cuban brand names and trademarks.

In the same declaration, supported by several countries and the European Union, Cuba considers Section 211 to be 'a unilateral measure of coercion contrary to international law and which represents an unprecedented extension and strengthening of the economic, financial and trade blockade'.

Even those opposed to the Cuban political system cannot deny that Section 211 is a rule made to measure for Bacardí-Martini and which has up to now only ever been used against Havana Rum and Liquors and its associate Pernod-Ricard.

It is important to mention that the amendment was introduced by the politicians Connie Mack and Robert Graham, the same people who had helped to push through the Torricelli-Graham Law and the Helms-Burton Law. What is more, there is an immense similarity in the terms set out in the amendment and a text that was presented to the Judicial Intellectual Property Subcommittee on 21 May 1998 by Ignacio Sánchez, the Bacardí lawyer and one of the authors of the Helms-Burton Law.

THE UNITED STATES HAS NOTHING TO SAY

Faced with the claims of Cuba and the European Union, the United States maintained that it had not violated international agreements with Section 211. On 2 December 1998 the Cuban government lodged a claim before the TRIPs Council against the United States in which it was demanded that they explain just how the amendment was not a violation of international treaties. Almost four months later, the US delegation presented the Council with copies of the Section together with a footnote saying that this information could be obtained on the Internet. In agreement with the European Union several countries said that this reply was inadequate. With their characteristic air of arrogance the delegation had misjudged the mood by saying that it would be happy to reply to any question on the subject as long as it was in writing ...[6]

MUCH MORE THAN JUST A RUM 'WAR'

On 4 February 2000, a US Court of Appeal issued a judgment that could have grave repercussions for international trade. It authorised the sale in the United States by Bacardí of a rum called Havana Club, protected by the Helms-Burton Act and Section 211. The decision went right up to the Supreme Court on appeal and the court upheld it. The EU then took the problem to the World Trade Organisation where a disputes panel found, in August 2001, against the law. The question was still unanswered, however, as to whether the US Congress would agree to change it. Throughout the dispute Bacardí kept threatening to produce a rum called Havana Club, but refrained from actually doing so.

However, what if Bacardí-Martini is ultimately able to acquire the right to own the brand name in the United States, contrary to every international convention? Since 1999, the Cuban government has indicated that these decisions by the US courts were forcing it to take reciprocal action. In other words, Cuba may revoke ownership rights to the more than 400 US trademarks registered there. What would happen if the drink Tropicola was canned as Coca-Cola? Or if fake McDonald's hamburger restaurants were set up in Varadero? It is certain that if Havana were to respond in this way, these two brands would foment another invasion of the island, or at least a total naval and air blockade. This is no joke or exaggeration. The most palpable demonstration of the seriousness of this situation came in March 2001 when President Castro announced that Cuba was to begin producing a rum called 'Bacardí', and of better quality (something that is easy for the Cubans to do). The news ran around the world and the State Department issued a categorical statement against it, calling it a grave provocation.[7]

Bacardí and the United States fly in the face of international regulations every time their own interests come into play. What is under the microscope here is not simply a struggle between Bacardí and the United States on the one hand and the Cuban government on the other. What they are doing is sabotaging the international rules that they themselves consider sacred, those that act to protect the ownership of trademarks. We are faced with a conflict in which all the weapons and tactics are at the service of the strongest in their mission to crush any resistance.

In the name of competition and private ownership the superpower and a mega monopoly are imposing the exact opposite. This is something which poses a grave danger to the system of globalisation of world markets, which needs at least a modicum of rules of engagement so as not to rush headlong over the precipice. Paradoxically Cuba, at the forefront in denouncing this crushing and enslaving system, is now at the centre of the argument.

Many of the US trademarks registered in Cuba (whose owners cannot mount a physical presence there due to the blockade imposed by their own government) are much more valuable than the network of factories, laboratories, offices and stores that they have all around the world. The value of brand names such as Coca-Cola and McDonald's is greater than the gross domestic product of several so-called Third World countries. Certainly better quality drinks exist than Coca-Cola (not to mention the McDonald's product), but their worth is founded in their recognition factor for the millions of consumers around the globe (these two are mentioned along with Bacardí as being amongst the ten most valuable on the planet).

This explains the vast sums spent on combating the counterfeit goods trade. If there is one thing feared by the owners of a prestigious brand it is piracy, not only in terms of lost sales but due to the inferior quality of the pirated product slowly destroying their image, turning regular customers away and alienating potential new ones. Is this what the multinational seeks? Because it should know that such a big lie to the consumer cannot be maintained for much longer.

14 Cuba's 'Transition' and 'Reconstruction'

CUBA'S 'RECONSTRUCTION'

As 1991 drew to a close, everything was being prepared for the fall of the Cuban revolution. Without the help of her old commercial partners from the ex-socialist bloc nothing could save her. In Miami, the many leaders of the diverse counter-revolutionary organisations argued aggressively and publicly over the distribution of government posts, starting with the presidency.

Meanwhile, the magnates whose property had been nationalised began packing their bags to be ready to leave as soon as the expected news was announced. The heads and shareholders of Bacardí expected to be among the small nucleus of the privileged allowed to safely take this route. This assumption was based on their close relationship with high-ranking US political movers and shakers, their powerful international business contacts, the efficient work undertaken behind the scenes with the CANF and, of course, their thousands of millions of dollars in capital.

It was therefore to be expected that they would favour the creation of the Blue Ribbon Commission on the Economic Reconstruction of Cuba. This commission was another branch of the CANF, an organisation with all the advantages to take control of the political situation in a post-revolutionary Cuba. No other group even came close to such power or acceptance by the US establishment.

The commission was launched as a 'project of political and economic transition', to study and come up with answers 'to the challenge of Cuban reconstruction'.[1] It was designed to collate information on key economic sectors in the island, formulating macroeconomic policies which would ultimately result in the imposition of a free market, neoliberal economy. The new government, according to this ambitious plan that had been formulated without taking into account anyone who lived on the island itself, would take no longer than two years to sell off all public assets. This privatisation would permit foreign companies to acquire up to 80 per cent of the shares irrespective of the sector chosen. It was a kind of bargain bucket shop sale.

Thomas Cox, a specialist in Latin America for the Heritage Foundation, was chairman of the commission. Malcolm Forbes, proprietor of *Forbes*, a publication aimed at the investor, acted as executive director. Also on the commission were Arthur Laffer, Reagan's favourite economist; William Clark of the National Security Council; and the politicians Robert Torricelli, Dante Fascell, Ileana Ros-Lethinen and Connie Mack, not to mention Jeanne Kirkpatrick and the AFL-CIO director William Doherty. The vice-chairman was Jorge Mas Canosa, head of the Cuban American National Foundation, who was setting himself up as future president in a post-revolutionary Cuba.

In no time at all, the commission attracted important multinationals on board. These, including Bell South, Coca-Cola, General Sugar, Chiquita and of course Bacardí, would receive preferential treatment when the privatisations went ahead, thanks to their support for the project from its inception.

SELLING OFF THE ISLAND

Ernesto Betancourt, ex-director of Radio Martí, wrote an article in *El Nuevo Herald* that was reproduced in the *New York Times*.[2] In it Betancourt completely rejected the Blue Ribbon Commission on the Economic Reconstruction of Cuba. But that was not all. He was also convinced that President George Bush Senior was wrong to support the CANF, an 'organisation whose leadership is dominated by ex-collaborators with the hated Batista dictatorship and their relatives'. A very sensitive charge, which says it all, but which no Bacardí shareholder in the Cuban American National Foundation asked to be retracted.

Elsewhere in the article, Betancourt expressed his opinion on the creation of the commission and its aims:

In its annual meeting [held in the spring], the Foundation announced the formation of a commission to draw up a plan for the economic reconstruction of Cuba [...]

Jeb Bush, son of the president, was the host; and ex-President Reagan was there to give his blessing [...]

If you were Cuban, would you not think that the United States was hatching a plan for Cuba's future and that the administration had chosen the Cuban American National Foundation to bring it about?

The group proclaims that it has purchasers wishing to pay $15,000,000 (sic), for 60 per cent of the land in Cuba and other assets.

Nobody gave the CANF the authority to sell off the island [...]

Although the leaders of the Foundation deny it, in private they are pleading for North American intervention [...][3]

FREE TRADE?

The *Miami Herald* stated that 'the businessmen in the Foundation are pragmatists. They know how to stay in the background as their leader [Jorge Mas Canosa] accepts all the platitudes whilst guaranteeing their aims [...]'[4] That is certainly the case. Right through the 1990s several Bacardí directors and shareholders took every opportunity to make their political and economic objectives for Cuba absolutely clear. Juan Grau left Cuba in the mid-1950s to go to Mexico where he was to assume the duties of second-in-command of the Bacardí distillery. A little while later he began to divide his duties for Bacardí with others in the country's oil industry. In the twelfth Hemisphere Congress of Chambers of Commerce and Latin American Industry that ended in Miami on 21 September 1991, Juan Grau, by now the head of Bacardí Import Inc., was awarded the title of businessman of the year. During his keynote speech he announced that free trade amongst the continent's nations was 'vital to a world order based on the honourable principle of "laissez faire" which could be roughly translated as meaning that when people buy and sell, governments should not interfere [...]'

Referring to the North American Free Trade Agreement (NAFTA) between Mexico, Canada and the United States, he stated that 'this will be the model for the future economic integration of the rest of Latin America'.[5]

The text of the Declaration of Principles by the Congress hoped that by 1992 'Cuba would be free' and would have accepted 'the concept of international trade'. It also supported the inevitability of privatisation of all state assets in Cuba and Latin America, and as a result backed the 'Initiative for the Americas' proposed by President George Bush.

It is worth remembering that the plan proposed by the US head of state in his 'Initiative' announced with much fanfare in the media in mid-1990, was based on the neoliberal theories which had become fashionable with the collapse of the socialist model in Eastern Bloc countries. It was also a politically inspired by the so-called think tanks, including the Heritage Foundation, and found voice in the following credo: 'A healthy democracy needs free commerce and the rule of market forces.'[6] A strange route to democracy.

'HUMANITARIAN' BUSINESSMEN

At the beginning of 1994, 'a Cuban American group of major businessmen and public figures' joined together in the Cuban Humanitarian Assistance Society to plan the delivery of large quantities of urgently needed aid to Cuba, 'as soon as a palpable move towards democracy and the free market comes about'. Although their members appeared ignorant of it, the Society's claims are somewhat contradictory though ultimately clear enough about its real objectives. 'The Society is an apolitical organisation, that is to say non-partisan and independent [...] It must be made absolutely clear that the Society is anti Castro [but] our categorical anti-Castro stance does not undermine but reinforces the Society's non-partisan nature, given that in the opposite case the Society would not be apolitical but simply and completely hypocritical.'[7]

A few days later the directors of the Society elaborated on these statements. In a press article entitled 'Businessmen announce Committee for the Reconstruction of Cuba', more details were given which would further negate the Society's humanitarian and apolitical nature, affirming instead their affinity with other extremist groups and the US strategy of destabilisation. The Society, it was said,

> [will be] an instrument of political pressure on the Cuban regime; and will furthermore call upon the United States

government to actively contribute with efforts to reconstruct the island after Castro [...] The Society could become an important player in the co-ordination of American aid to Cuba [...] Other organisations that have developed plans to send aid to Cuba, such as Brothers to the Rescue and the Cuban American National Foundation, could co-ordinate their efforts through the Society.

The most well-known businessman in the Cuban Humanitarian Assistance Society was Juan Grau, who is, as we already know, one of the highest-ranking Bacardí directors.

THE US-CUBA BUSINESS COUNCIL

In November 1993, the US-Cuba Business Council was formed, nearly three years after the Foundation's Blue Ribbon Commission on the Economic Reconstruction of Cuba. The aims of both organisations were almost identical, with the exception that those of the Council did not contain the provisos that had upset and hurt several Cubans in the United States and Europe. The Council did not propose to sell off '60 per cent of the land in Cuba and other assets' as Ernesto Betancourt had stated when referring to the Commission. It did not mention sell-offs or percentages, but its intentions went further, although couched in rather more subtle terms. From the date of its official registration in Washington its objectives have remained the same and have only been conditioned by the requirements of US policy towards Cuba.

Declaring itself to be a non-profit organisation, the governing body of the Council basically consists of US nationals, and as it states in its own documents:

with notable diplomatic and political experience, both at international level and in the business sphere. Together they represent years of experience in Cuban affairs. The Council has access to a wide range of prominent experts and consultants on the subjects of development and businesses in Cuba.

Apparently none of these 'experts' live in Cuba.

Some of the companies that go to make up the Council include Bacardí, Kelley Drye & Warren, Chiquita, Coca-Cola, Colgate Palmolive, Ford Motors, General Motors, The *Miami Herald*, Pepsi-Cola, Texaco, Amstar, and so on.

The principal slogan of the Business Council is: 'Preparing for trade and investment in a democratic free market Cuba.'[8] Composed of corporations which in the main have claims against the Cuban government as a result of nationalisations, the Council 'supports current US policy on Cuba, designed to foster a democratic change with guarantees of freedom and human rights, under the rule of law'.

The aims of the US-Cuba Business Council are to '[...] promote cooperation among business, civic and professional organisations which share our goals for democracy and a market economy in Cuba'. This 'cooperation' is a crucial advance in the Council's proposals:

> Upon resumption of US laws and regulations on Cuba, provide timely research; develop a network of business sources interested in commercial opportunities on the island; co-ordinate participation in US humanitarian aid trade development programs; educate Cuban citizens about the benefits of a free market economy [...]

Apart from a word or two, are these not the same words as those proposed by the Cuban American National Foundation and all those organisations that push for a Cuba à la Puerto Rico: a pseudo US colony?

IS BACARDÍ 'MAKING' THE ECONOMIC TRANSITION?

If tomorrow, for instance, the Cuban Revolution was to come to an end, there would be several counter-revolutionary leaders around to begin arguing over their jobs in a carnival atmosphere reminiscent of the times of the collapse of the European socialist camp. And although their undisputed leader, Jorge Mas Canosa, died in November 1997, nevertheless the members and associates of the Foundation continue to be those best placed to take the reins of governmental power. It goes without saying that they would have to subscribe to the diktat of the Helms-Burton Law, as this is what determines how such a transition process would take place from beginning to end.

And at present, irrespective of those figures accepted by Washington to front the transition, and before the recognition of any post-revolutionary government, the Helms-Burton Law orders the president to create a very peculiar organisation which must become a key player in the economic restructuring of the new state; and Article 203 of the Helms-Burton Law states that it should be called the US-Cuba Council, charged with:

1. Guaranteeing that there is co-ordination between government activities and those of the private sector designed to respond to changes that have occurred in Cuba and to promote development on the island based on the market.
2. Holding regular meetings between representatives of the private sector in the United States and Cuba with the aim of promoting bilateral trade.

Otto Reich maintains that the designation of a Business Council 'is a routine and straightforward matter whenever the United States becomes a partner in a structured agreement with another country'.[9]

The anomaly in this instance, according to the same journalistic source, was that the Cuban revolutionary state was still in existence, yet the Council had already been set up 'administered by Otto Reich [...]' It is an amazing coincidence that Reich, a Council founder member, was the same person who participated in drafting the Helms-Burton Bill on behalf of the Bacardí multinational.

There are other names involved in the symbiosis between Bacardí, the Business Council and the Helms-Burton Act. Robert Freer Jr, founder member and currently the Council's executive secretary, also had a hand in the Act. As did the lawyer Ignacio Sánchez, a member of Kelley Drye & Warren, the legal firm employed by Bacardí and which sits on the Council. Another founder member and currently vice-president of the Council is Thomas Cox, consultant for the Heritage Foundation and ex-co-ordinator for the Blue Ribbon Commission on the Economic Reconstruction of Cuba set up by the Cuban American National Foundation. Another founder member is Juan Prado, the well-known Bacardí shareholder and director as well as a prominent member of Cuba On-Line.[10]

Then there is Manuel J. Cutillas, patriarch of the Bacardí empire, trustee of the Cuban American National Foundation, honorary Mexican consul in the Bahamas, ex-director of the Mexican TV conglomerate Televisa and one of the governors of the temple to capitalist tyranny that is the World Economic Forum (the Davos Summit).[11] Cutillas was also the chief founder of the Business Council, currently holding the title of Emeritus Executive President. The same Cutillas who 'has been involved in efforts to hasten the demise of the Castro regime [...]'[12]

'CUBA IN TRANSITION'

The Helms-Burton Act also requires the US president to implement a plan to deliver economic assistance to a Cuba 'in transition'. In spite of the fact that this is yet to come, the Business Council already receives finance from the National Endowment for Democracy and the United States Agency for International Development (USAID), designed to advance the 'Cuba transition' programme and ultimately 'assist the United States government in this effort'. Until now 'the US-Cuba Business Council has been the only business association participating in this initiative so significant for the US government', as the Council's publicity material continually states. To assist in this, in 1997, the USAID gave it $567,000. It had previously obtained $300,000 for its 'experts' to hold 'meetings on the Cuban economy and assistance to Cuban democracy, aimed at the private sector'.

To sum up, the 'Cuba transition' programme includes surveys of major US corporations regarding post-embargo investment and trade; studies on key industries in Cuba and future development requirements; conferences debating the future of Cuba; reports on current foreign holdings and joint venture investment initiatives in Cuba, as well as established claims resulting from confiscation, and so forth.

And that's not all. The Council has included among its aims that of requesting from its member companies: 'food, medicine and other goods' to deliver to the Cuban people. Although this should not happen until the transition has begun, this 'assistance programme' too already appears to be under way. Its aim is not so much humanitarian but rather to assist 'American companies to establish a positive identity as a contributor to socio-economic development in a free market Cuba'.

WILL BACARDÍ BE PUT IN CHARGE OF SELLING OFF CUBA?

If events happen as planned, the US-Cuba Business Council will be the real power in a post-revolutionary Cuba as co-ordinators of the principal aim of the Helms-Burton Act: the auctioning off and appropriation of the island by US and especially Cuban-American corporations.

A combination of everything already outlined, together with the madness provoked by the money sloshing around the US legislative system, means that the directors or representatives of a company not even based in the country itself would be at the forefront of this process.

If that happens those companies that have been 'trafficking' in nationalised property will have to pay a hefty price for their temerity, both in terms of the amount of time already spent there and the right to stay. For example, Pernod-Ricard will have to pay for every bottle it has put on the shelves and Sol-Meliá for the tourists it has accommodated. If not they will be thrown out.

This is the dream that Bacardí and the United States have committed to paper. Reality, however, is not that simple; every day there is more and more foreign investment in Cuba. If the capitalist system and its globalisation were to come about on the island it would witness a confrontation of unimaginable proportions.

BACKDROP

As a fanatical servant of US interests, Bacardí offers Cuba the prospect of semi-colonial status. As a lover of the tyranny of naked capitalism, Bacardí-Martini promises to convert Cuba into a duty-free zone.

An 'over the top' assessment? As this work draws to an end the words of Eduardo Sardiña, one of the most prominent of Bacardí's directors, can serve as a backdrop: 'If the United States recognises Cuba and conditions for business are favourable then Bacardí might seriously consider returning to Cuba.'[13]

... If the US ... and conditions are favourable ...
No comment necessary. Just a pause for breath ...

Postscript

The Cuban American National Foundation and the Center for a Free Cuba are two registered organisations in the United States. They have several facets in common: they claim to be non-profit making, independent and non-partisan, aiming to inform at an international level on the political, economic and human rights situation in Cuba. They are all designed, according to their publicity, to bring about the downfall of the Cuban revolutionary process. These organisations also share another crucial factor in common. Not only do they receive finance from Bacardí but representatives of the rum multinational also sit on their governing bodies.

For example, Clara María del Valle, a Bacardí shareholder whose father formed part of the mercenary forces that landed in the Bay of Pigs and who promoted the Miami paramilitary organisation, the Cuban Representation in Exile, has been one of the foremost activists in the work conducted by the Cuban American National Foundation in the field of human rights. In this she has worked extensively with Luis Zúñiga, who in 1974 was detained by Cuban security forces as he attempted to infiltrate the island to commit acts of terrorism. Señora del Valle is currently vice-president of the Cuban American National Foundation: and she was one of those who signed the Foundation's public letter of support for the bombing of several Cuban hotels in 1997 which injured a number of people and killed an Italian businessman (incidentally the country of origin of Martini, now part of the Bacardí consortium). This proclamation was also signed by Ignacio Sánchez, also a CANF director and one of Bacardí's principal lawyers as well as being one of the authors of the Helms-Burton Bill.

However, one must not forget that the governing body of the Cuban American National Foundation also contains four other Bacardí shareholders, among them the patriarch of the company, Manuel Cutillas. Nor must it be overlooked that the bombings were masterminded by the terrorist Luis Posada Carriles who had received CANF cash many times in the past, as he himself declared to the *New York Times*. But the campaign for 'human rights' by the CANF is not something that is isolated. Ever since Ronald Reagan signed National Security Directive No. 17 in 1981, which specified the importance of working with 'the Cuban community in exile' in order to 'develop public pressure against Cuba, highlighting human rights and political matters', many groups and individuals of the extreme right have united under this flag.

One of the very first was Frank Calzón who, as has been shown earlier in this book, arrived on the scene via terrorist organisations backed up and controlled by the CIA. Calzón has been a member of Freedom House and of Human Reach, as well as the first ever chairman of the Cuban American National Foundation. Currently Calzón is director of the Center for a Free Cuba which is also financed by the National Endowment for Democracy, and whose directors include the ex-ambassador Jeanne Kirkpatrick, George W. Bush's choice as spokesman on Latin American Affairs, Otto Reich, William Doherty. Modesto Maidique and Luis Aguilar León, among others, all of whom have links with the US security services and counter-revolutionary plans. Furthermore, the chairman of the Center is Manuel J. Cutillas, CANF director and overall head of Bacardí.

In its work with Europe, the Center collaborates closely with the Catholic organisation Pax Christi in Holland, supported in good part by its International Secretariat.

Both the CANF and the Center for a Free Cuba, in addition to these 'coincidences' were the ones who made more lobbying efforts than any other to try and ensure that the child Elián González remained illegally detained in the United States, contrary to the wishes of international law and those of his father living in Cuba. When the child was finally handed over to his father more than 20 émigré organisations in Miami, led by the CANF, joined in the protests to paralyse Miami on 25 April 2000. According to the EFE news agency, the vice president of Bacardí, Jorge Rodríguez, announced: 'As a member of the Cuban community and in recognition of this tragic moment, the company will close.'

Appendix: Diagrams

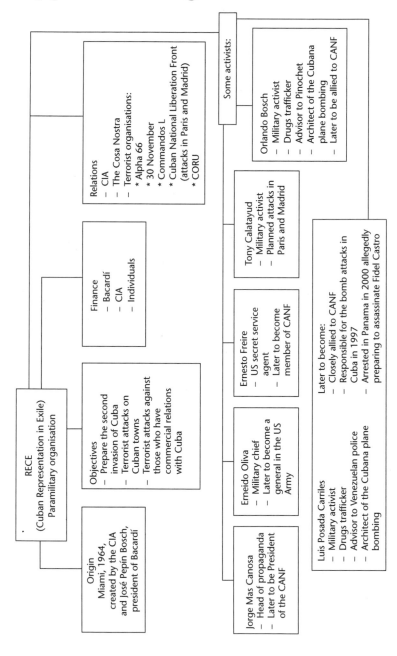

RECE
(Cuban Representation in Exile)
Paramilitary organisation

Origin
Miami, 1964,
created by the CIA
and José Pepín Bosch,
president of Bacardí

Objectives
– Prepare the second
  invasion of Cuba
– Terrorist attacks on
  Cuban towns
– Terrorist attacks against
  those who have
  commercial relations
  with Cuba

Finance
– Bacardí
– CIA
– Individuals

Relations
– CIA
– The Cosa Nostra
– Terrorist organisations:
  * Alpha 66
  * 30 November
  * Commandos L
  * Cuban National Liberation Front
    (attacks in Paris and Madrid)
  * CORU

Some activists:

Orlando Bosch
– Military activist
– Drugs trafficker
– Advisor to Pinochet
– Architect of the Cubana
  plane bombing
– Later to be allied to CANF

Tony Calatayud
– Military activist
– Planned attacks in
  Paris and Madrid

Ernesto Freire
– US secret service
  agent
– Later to become
  member of CANF

Erneido Oliva
– Military chief
– Later to become a
  general in the US
  Army

Jorge Mas Canosa
– Head of propaganda
– Later to be President
  of the CANF

Luis Posada Carriles
– Military activist
– Drugs trafficker
– Advisor to Venezuelan police
– Architect of the Cubana plane
  bombing

Later to become:
– Closely allied to CANF
– Responsible for the bomb attacks in
  Cuba in 1997
– Arrested in Panama in 2000 allegedly
  preparing to assassinate Fidel Castro

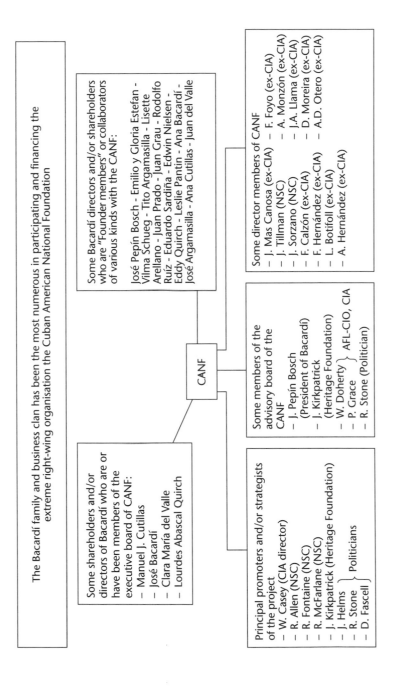

The Bacardí family and business clan has been the most numerous in participating and financing the extreme right-wing organisation the Cuban American National Foundation

Some shareholders and/or directors of Bacardí who are or have been members of the executive board of CANF:
- Manuel J. Cutillas
- José Bacardí
- Clara María del Valle
- Lourdes Abascal Quirch

Some Bacardí directors and/or shareholders who are "Founder members" or collaborators of various kinds with the CANF:

José Pepín Bosch - Emilio y Gloria Estefan - Vilma Schueg - Tito Argamasilla - Lisette Arellano - Juan Prado - Juan Grau - Rodolfo Ruíz - Eduardo Sardiña - Edwin Nielsen - Eddy Quirch - Leslie Pantin - Ana Bacardí - José Argamasilla - Ana Cutillas - Juan del Valle

CANF

Some director members of CANF
- J. Mas Canosa (ex-CIA)   - F. Foyo (ex-CIA)
- J. Tillman (NSC)   - A. Monzón (ex-CIA)
- J. Sorzano (NSC)   - J.A. Llama (ex-CIA)
- F. Calzón (ex-CIA)   - D. Moreira (ex-CIA)
- F. Hernández (ex-CIA)   - A.D. Otero (ex-CIA)
- L. Botifoll (ex-CIA)
- A. Hernández (ex-CIA)

Some members of the advisory board of the CANF
- J. Pepín Bosch (President of Bacardí)
- J. Kirkpatrick (Heritage Foundation)
- W. Doherty } AFL-CIO, CIA
- P. Grace
- R. Stone (Politician)

Principal promoters and/or strategists of the project
- W. Casey (CIA director)
- R. Allen (NSC)
- R. Fontaine (NSC)
- R. McFarlane (NSC)
- J. Kirkpatrick (Heritage Foundation)
- J. Helms
- R. Stone } Politicians
- D. Fascell

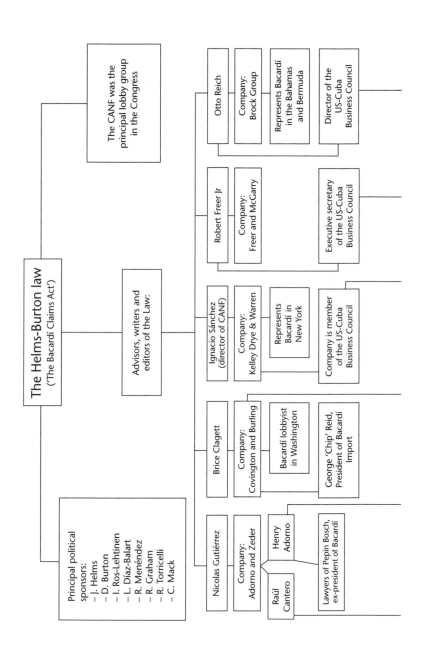

The Helms-Burton law
('The Bacardí Claims Act')

Principal political sponsors:
– J. Helms
– D. Burton
– I. Ros-Lehtinen
– L. Díaz-Balart
– R. Menéndez
– R. Graham
– R. Torricelli
– C. Mack

The CANF was the principal lobby group in the Congress

Advisors, writers and editors of the Law:

Nicolas Gutiérrez

Company: Adorno and Zeder

Raúl Cantero

Henry Adorno

Lawyers of Pepín Bosch, ex-president of Bacardí

Brice Clagett

Company: Covington and Burling

Bacardí lobbyist in Washington

George 'Chip' Reid, President of Bacardí Import

Ignacio Sánchez (director of CANF)

Company: Kelley Drye & Warren

Represents Bacardí in New York

Company is member of the US-Cuba Business Council

Robert Freer Jr

Company: Freer and McGarry

Executive secretary of the US-Cuba Business Council

Otto Reich

Company: Brock Group

Represents Bacardí in the Bahamas and Bermuda

Director of the US-Cuba Business Council

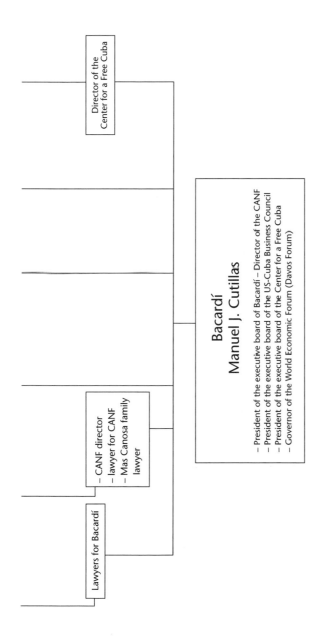

Lawyers for Bacardí

- CANF director
- lawyer for CANF
- Mas Canosa family lawyer

Director of the Center for a Free Cuba

Bacardí
Manuel J. Cutillas

- President of the executive board of Bacardí – Director of the CANF
- President of the executive board of the US–Cuba Business Council
- President of the executive board of the Center for a Free Cuba
- Governor of the World Economic Forum (Davos Forum)

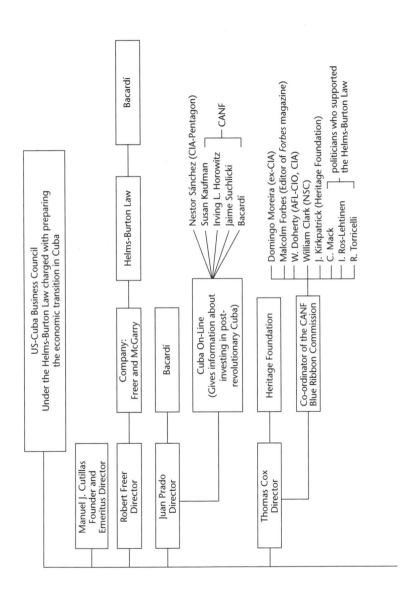

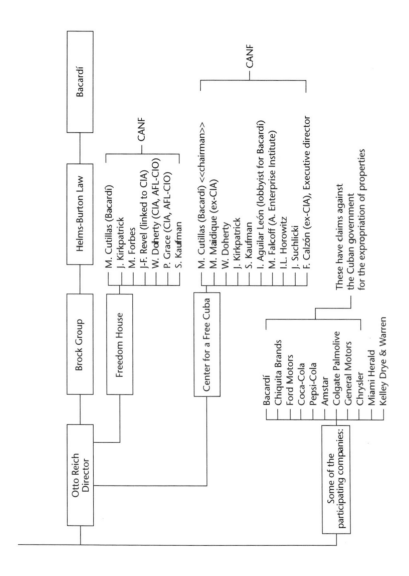

Notes

INTRODUCTION

1. America is a continent, not a country. It is incorrect to call the citizens of a country called the United States 'Americans'. Equally it is a mistake to call them 'North Americans' because Canada, and according to some, Mexico also belong to that continent. For this reason the author will use 'US' to denominate all that which pertains to this country and its inhabitants. However, he will respect the terms used in quotations and references. *(All notes with the exception of those indicated to the contrary are by the author.)*
2. *El Nuevo Herald*, Miami, 21 January 2000.

CHAPTER 1

1. Hurtado, Nicolás Torres, *Orígenes de la Compañía Bacardí*, Santiago de Cuba, 1977. Photocopy. Publisher unknown. In this work, the author uses dates and figures from the official accounts of the *Sociedad Bacardí-Bouteiller* and the later *Compañía Bacardí*. He quotes precisely the results and annual balances of the company from 1880 to 1919. He also cites other results from the company between 1920 and 1954.
2. *The World of Bacardí-Martini*, edited for Bacardí Limited-PemBrocke, Bermuda, by Sidney M. Maran. There is no precise date for the publication but it was certainly during the 1990s.
3. Ibid.

CHAPTER 2

1. Hurtado, Nicolás Torres, *Orígenes de la Compañía Bacardí*, Santiago de Cuba, 1977, photocopy.
2. Ibid.
3. Gosch, Martin and Hammer, Richard, *Lucky Luciano: Le Testament*, Stock, Paris, 1975.
4. Ibid.
5. *The World of Bacardí-Martini*.
6. *The World of Bacardí Museum*, Bacardí-Martini USA Inc., Miami, 1996.
7. Torras, Jacinto, *Hoy* newspaper, Havana, 24 April 1943.
8. Torras, Jacinto, *Hoy* newspaper, Havana, 8 June 1944.
9. *The World of Bacardí-Martini*.
10. Cirules, Enrique, *El imperio de La Habana*, Casa de las Américas, Havana, 1993.

11. Cervera, Jesús Arboleya, *La contrarrevolución Cubana*, Ciencias Sociales, Havana, 1997.
12. Cirules, *El imperio de La Habana*.

CHAPTER 3

1. Benes, Alejando, 'The Spirit of the Bat', *Cigar Aficionado*, Washington, 1996.
2. *The World of Bacardí-Martini*.
3. Ibid.
4. Smith, Earl, *The Fourth Floor*, Random House, New York, 1962.
5. Kiger, Patrick and Kruger, John, 'Squeeze Play: The United States, Cuba, and the Helms-Burton Act', *The Center for Public Integrity*, Washington, March 1997.
6. Franqui, Carlos, *Vida, aventuras y desastres de un hombre llamado Castro*, Planeta, Barcelona, 1978.
7. Bernard, Chenot, *Les entreprises nationalisées*, Presses Universitaires de France, Paris, 1977. At the time of the Cuban revolution, the state economies in France and England for example, were only surpassed by the Soviet Union and the other countries of the European socialist bloc. The strategic sectors of the economy were all nationalised.
8. Benes, Alejandro, 'The Spirit of the Bat'.
9. Ibid.
10. *The World of Bacardí-Martini*.

CHAPTER 4

1. Vargas Llosa, Álvaro, *El Exilio Indomable*, Espasa-Calpe, Madrid, 1998. This book, as the author makes clear in the opening pages, was written by request of the Cuban American National Foundation, a far-right organisation based in Miami, but the final result is self-revelatory. Among the people who offer testimony to the author is the Bacardí shareholder and director of the Foundation, Clara María de la Valle.
2. Ibid.
3. Ibid.
4. Rasco, José Ignacio, 'Orígenes de la Brigada 2506', *El Nuevo Herald*, Miami, 24 April 1997. See also 'Restored B-26 to honor Bay of Pigs pilots', *Miami Herald*, 30 March 2000. The article says that on 15 April a memorial installed by the Association of Cuban pilots in Miami would be inaugurated representing ex-mercenaries of the Bay of Pigs. The memorial would be a plane donated by the US Air Force museum. The transfer of the plane from California would cost $25,000, which would be covered by Bacardí, according to the source.
5. Vargas Llosa, Álvaro, *El Exilio Indomable*.
6. *United States Position on Efforts by Cuban Exiles to Achieve*, Memo From Gordon Chase of the National Security Council Staff to the President's Special Assistant for National Security Affairs, Washington, 28 May 1963. The NSC comprises the Secretaries of State and Defense, the

National Security Adviser, the Director of the CIA, three White House advisers and the Attorney-General.

7. Bardach, Ann Louise, 'Cuba: The Beginning of the End', *The New Republic*, Washington, 3 October 1994.
8. Johnson, Haynes, *La Baie des Cochons. L'invasion manquée de Cuba*, Robert Laffont, Paris, 1965.
9. Encinosa, Enrique, *Cuba en guerra. Historia de la oposicón anti-castrista 1959–1993*, The Endowment for Cuban American Studies of the Cuban American National Foundation, Miami, 1995.
10. Vargas Llosa, Álvaro, *El Exilio Indomable*.
11. Rivero Collado, Carlos, *Los sobrinos de tío Sam*, Akal, Madrid, 1977.
12. According to the former member of the Brigade 2506, Carlos Rivero Collado, in his work cited above, from 1964 to 1974, 'Delegations of RECE, organised in all the centres of the emigration, collected several million dollars. This capital has been invested in bank operations and mainly in the acquisition of lands and property based in Florida. Thus, for example, Ernesto Freire is the executive vice-president of the Jefferson National Bank of Miami Beach. Jorge Mas Canosa is one of the biggest shareholders in the powerful real estate company, Keyes Realty Corporation (in which Carlos Prío Socarrás and the close friend of Nixon, Bebe Rebozo also have shares). Keyes Realty owns big areas of land and urban lots in the southern zone of Dade County. Tony Calatayud used his share of the money to buy the radio stations WRIZ and Radio World and to invest in real estate in association with Mas Canosa. Erneido Oliva, in recompense for his work in RECE, received a house valued at more than $50,000 in Washington DC.'
13. Gaeton Fonzi, who has worked as an investigator for special Commissions of the US Congress, publishes this information in two works: *The Last Investigation*, Thunder's Mouth Press, New York, 1993, and 'Who is Jorge Mas Canosa?', *Esquire*, January 1993.
14. Fonzi, Gaeton, 'Who is Jorge Mas Canosa?'
15. 'Memorandum to McGeorge Bundy from Gordon Chase. Subject: Assassination of Castro', The White House, Washington, 15 June 1965. The report that accompanies the letter: 'Memorandum for: The Director of Central Intelligence. Subject: Plans of Cuban Exiles to Assassinate Selected Cuban Government Leaders', 10 June 1964.
16. Vargas Llosa, Álvaro, *El Exilio Indomable*.
17. Talleda, Miguel, *Alpha 66 y su histórica tarea*, Universal Miami, 1995. See also Calvo Ospina, Hernando and Declercq, Katlijn, *The Cuban Exile Movement. Dissidents or Mercenaries?* Ocean Press, Melbourne and New York, 2000.
18. Llosa, Álvaro Vargas, *El Exilio Indomable*. The terrorist organisations Alpha 66, 30 November and Commando L were the first with whom RECE worked. They were so radical that the US authorities, including the CIA, called them 'causes for attention' (see Enrique Encinosa, *Cuba en guerra*).
19. Ibid.
20. Ibid.
21. Ibid.

CHAPTER 5

1. In the US think tanks are non-profit foundations or research centres that work on public policy proposals.
2. Vargas Llosa, Álvaro, *El Exilio Indomable*.
3. Dinges, John and Landau, Saul, *Assassination on Embassy Row*, Pantheon Books, New York, 1980.
4. Kiger, Patrick and Kruger, John, 'Squeeze Play'.
5. Encinosa, Enrique, *Cuba en guerra. Historia de la oposición anti-castrista 1959–93*.
6. Labrousse, Alain, 'Les obscurs destins de l'argent de la drogue', *Le Monde Diplomatique*, Paris, January 1992.
7. Arboleya Cervera, Jesús, *La contrarrevolución cubana*, Ciencias Sociales, Havana, 1997.
8. Fonzi, Gaeton, 'Who is Jorge Mas Canosa?'
9. Vargas Llosa, Álvaro, *El Exilio Indomable*.
10. Encinosa, Enrique, *Cuba en guerra*.
11. Vargas Llosa, Álvaro, *El Exilio Indomable*.

CHAPTER 6

1. Fonzi, Gaeton, 'Who is Jorge Mas Canosa?'
2. Dale Scott, Peter and Marshall, Jonathan, *Cocaine Politics. Drugs, Armies, and the CIA in Central America*, University of California Press, Berkeley, Los Angeles, Oxford, 1991. This highly respected book details the participation of Cuban counter-revolutionaries in the traffic of drugs during the anti-Sandinista war. It confirms that many of them already had experience in the matter. The names of Posada Carriles and Orlando Bosch, among other terrorists, stand out in this work as do economic contributory organisations such as CORU and the CNLF, umbrella organisations that formed part of RECE.
3. Fonzi, Gaeton, 'Who is Jorge Mas Canosa?'
4. There is a vast documentation on 'Project Democracy' and the people involved in it, for example, The Kerry Report, 'Drugs, Law Enforcement and Foreign Policy', Subcommittee on Terrorism, Narcotics and International Operations of Foreign Relations, United States Senate, US Government Printing Office, Washington, 1989; Hunter Marshall, Scott, *The Iran Contra Connection. Secret Themes and Covert Operations in the Reagan Era*, South End, Boston, 1985.
5. Joel Woldman: *The National Endowment for Democracy, Foreign Affairs and National Defense Division*, Congressional Research Service, Washington, June 1985.
6. Vargas Llosa, Álvaro, *El Exilio Indomable*.
7. Fonzi, Gaeton, 'Who is Jorge Mas Canosa?'
8. Ibid.
9. Vargas Llosa, Álvaro, *El Exilio Indomable*.
10. 'A New Inter-American Policy for the Eighties', better known as the Santa Fe Document, was produced for a special committee of US

politicians, investigators and military. It offered an analysis and recommendations on the foreign policy of the United States that formed the basis of action for the Reagan administration.

11. Evron Kirkpatrick, husband of the ambassador, was one of the most important founders of the CIA. Among his highly secret activities was his participation in the National Psychological Warfare Program, which resulted in the persecution of intellectuals and artists for their presumed relationship with the international communism. (See Hatch, Richard and Diamond, Sara, 'Operation Peace Institute', *Z Magazine*, Boston, July–August 1990.)

12. Vargas Llosa, Álvaro, *El Exilo Indominable*.

CHAPTER 7

1. Philip Agee, ex-CIA officer, in his book *Journal d'un agent secret* (Editions du Seuil, Paris, 1976), a book which has caused him to suffer reprisals at the hands of the US government, accused Doherty of being a 'union infiltrator from the CIA' whilst simultaneously a director of AIFLD. Grace, as president of W R Grace and Co., a multinational with a strong presence in Latin America, is fingered as an 'important collaborator with the CIA in its union operations'. To our knowledge this has never been denied.

2. Other figures of the Bacardí 'family' maintaining various links, and/or financing the Foundation or other anti-Cuban activities; be they resident in the US, Mexico, Puerto Rico or the Bahamas, include: Emilio and Gloria Estefan, Eddy Quirch, Leslie Pantin, Ana María Bacardí Comas, Tito Argamasilla Bacardí, José Argamasilla Grimany, Vilma Schueg Arellano, Lissette Arellano, Ana María Cutillas, Juan M. del Valle, etc. References to these can be found in *Fundación*, the Foundation's journal, which published this list as 'humble recognition of those men amongst the CANF membership who have loyally made their contributions through the years and have been admitted to the category of founder member'.

3. 'Homenaje de Bacardí a Luis Aguilar León', *Diario Las Américas*, Miami, 22 June 1996. See also Llosa, Álvaro Vargas, *El Exilio Indomable*.

4. Gresh, Alain, 'Une sainte alliance contre l'insaisissable ennemi?', *Le Monde Diplomatique*, Paris, February 1987. Ravel has been on the Board of Freedom House, an organisation claiming to be pro-human rights, but somewhat biased towards US political interests.

5. 'Vargas Llosa supports the embargo against Castro', *Diario Las Américas*, Miami, 22 February 1994.

6. *El Nuevo Herald*, Miami, 11 October 1991.

7. 'Por Una Cuba Libre y Democrática' ('For a Free and Democratic Cuba'), *Fundación*, CANF news publication, Miami, May 1998. See also Calvo Ospina, Hernando and Declercq, Katlijn, *Dissidents or Mercenaries? The Cuban Exile Movement*, Ocean Press, Melbourne–New York, 2000.

8. *El Nuevo Herald*, Miami, 4 April 1992. 'Interview with Hubert Matos' and 'Interview with Ricardo Bofill'. See Calvo Ospina and Declercq, *Dissidents or Mercenaries? The Cuba Exile Movement*.

9. 'For a Free and Democratic Cuba', Cuban American National Foundation, Miami. Exact date of publication unclear, although most probably at the beginning of the 1990s. Luis Aguilar León formed part of the select, tight-knit group working on Radio Swan in 1960. This was a clandestine CIA station aimed at Cuba and specialising in propaganda. Other intellectuals linked with ECAS include Susan Kaufman (Freedom House), Mark Falcoff (Freedom House and the American Enterprise Institute), Paul Hollander, Irving L. Horowitz and James Suchlicki, among others.
10. Vargas Llosa, Álvaro, *El Exilio Indomable.*
11. In May 2000, this centre of education awarded Cutillas a degree. In 1993 they had already given this honour to the singer Gloria Estefan, who is also a member of the Bacardí 'clan'.
12. Pérez Castellón, Ninoska, *Un hombre y su tiempo* (A Man and His Times), Cuban American National Foundation, Miami, July 1998.
13. Ibid.
14. Encinosa, Enrique, *Cuba en guerra, Historia de la oposición anti-castrista 1959–1993* (Cuba at War. History of the anti-Castro Opposition 1959–1993).
15. *Diario Las Américas*, Miami, 17 March 1992.
16. 'Carta abierta al presidente de los Estados Unidos: Los días de castro están contados. 'No rescate a su dictadura fracasada!' advertisement, *El Nuevo Herald*, 27 September 1994. 'Citizens for a Free Cuba' included figures such as: Ambassador Jeanne Kirkpatrick, Under-Secretary of State Elliot Abrams, William Clark of the National Security Council; as well as the Cuban-American ambassadors Otto Reich and José Sorzano, among others. Other signatories included various members of the Foundation, Cuban-American sugar magnates, and so on. But the vast majority of signatures on the 'Open Letter' were members of the Bacardí 'family', among them Manuel J. Cutillas, Juan Grau, Juan Prado, Edwin Nielsen, various Arellano family members, Leslie Pantin and Eddy Quirch.

CHAPTER 8

1. On 10 October 1994, with the Boland Amendment, Congress had decided to deny military aid to the Contras as well as prohibiting the conduct of direct or indirect military or paramilitary operations against Nicaragua by the Reagan administration.
2. Kerry Report, 'Drugs, Law Enforcement and Foreign Policy', Subcommittee on Terrorism, Narcotics and International Operations of Foreign Relations, United States Senate, US Government Printing Office, Washington, 1989.
3. Calvo Ospina, Hernando, *Don Pablo et ses amis*, EPO, Brussels, 1994.
4. Ramonet, Ignacio, 'La longue guerre oculte contre le Nicaragua', *Le Monde Diplomatique*, Paris, February 1987.
5. The Frenchmen Bernard-Henry Lévy and Jean François Revel were among those who signed a letter sent to the US Congress in which aid and funds were called upon for the Contras. Among the main private

organisations or 'think tanks', lending assistance to the National Security Council and the State Department in the Contras war were: the Cuban American National Foundation; the National Defense Council and the Foundation Conservative Caucus: within the governing body of which were the ex-military leaders John Singlaub and Daniel Graham, as well as Jesse Helms and Dan Burton, lawmakers united for the first time in a counter-revolutionary project; the Order of Malta; the Heritage Foundation; AFL-CIO; Freedom House; the American Enterprise Institute; the US Security Council, counting amongst its members the lawmakers Jesse Helms and Robert Dole in addition to D. Graham and J. Singlaub; the World Anti-Communist League headed by J. Singlaub; Friends of the Democratic Center in Central America, among whose activists were W. Doherty, P. Grace, J. Kirkpatrick, J. Mas Canosa, and so on.

6. Posada Carriles, Luis, *Los caminos del guerrero*, edited by the author, 1994. See also Ann Louise Bardach and Larry Rother, 'Authorities knew of bombing attacks says exile', *New York Times*, New York, 12 July 1998.
7. The Kerry Report, 'Drugs, Law Enforcement and Foreign Policy', Also see Dale, Peter and Marshall, Jonathan, *Cocaine Politics, Drugs, Armies and the CIA in Central America*.
8. 'CANF achievements. Assistance to freedom fighters', *Miami Herald*, advertisement, Miami, 20 May 1986.
9. Ibid.
10. Vargas Llosa, Álvaro, *El Exilio Indomable*.
11. Fonzi, Geaton, 'Who is Jorge Mas Canosa?'
12. Posada Carriles, Luis, *Los Caminos del guerrero*.
13. Fonzi, Gaeton, 'Who is Jorge Mas Canosa?'
14. Posada Carriles, Luis, *Los Caminos del guerrero*.
15. Bacelar, Ruy, 'Les appuis de l'Unita', *Le Monde Diplomatique*, Paris, June 1991.
16. Faligot, Roger, 'Services secrets en Afrique', *Le Sycomore*, Paris, 1982.
17. Office of the legislator Frank Church, US Senate, US Government Printing Office, Washington, 1975.
18. Faligot, Roger, 'Services secrets en Afrique'.
19. Black Manafort, Stone and Kelly have also had the account of the ousted dictator Mobuto, with whom he signed in 1989 a $1 million contract to seek aid from the US government.
20. Vargas Llosa, Álvaro, *El Exilio Indomable*.
21. It is not necessary to mention again here the conservative groups instrumental in providing assistance to UNITA, given that they were also those aiding the Contras and are already outlined in note 5.
22. John Stockwell was the figure that the CIA placed at the head of the Angolan Task Force to direct the secret war. Years later Stockwell would admit that Cuba had not received the order to intervene from the Soviet Union. On the contrary, 'the Cuban leadership felt obliged to intervene in Angola for their own ideological reasons' (Faligot, Roger, 'Services secrets en Afrique').
23. Vargas Llosa, Álvaro, *El Exilio Indomable*.
24. Abramovici, Pierre, 'Des millions de dollars pour les "combatants de la liberté"', *Le Monde Diplomatique*, Paris, April 1986.

25. 'Logros de la FNCA. Ayuda a los combatientes por la libertad', *Miami Herald*, advertisement, Miami, 20 May 1986.
26. 'La Fundación Informa al pueblo', *Diario Las Américas*, advertisement, Miami, 20 May 1988.
27. *Jornal de Angola*, Luanda, 15 January 1999.

CHAPTER 9

1. *El Nuevo Herald*, Miami, 26 September 1992.
2. Vargas Llosa, Álvaro, *El Exilio Indomable*.
3. Pérez Castellón, Ninoska, *Un hombre y su tiempo*.
4. Vargas Llosa, Álvaro, *El Exilio Indomable*.
5. In bold in the original.
6. *Diario Las Américas*, Miami, 30 January 1992.
7. *Wall Street Journal*, New York, 16 October 1992.
8. Vargas Llosa, Álvaro, *El Exilio Indomable*.
9. *Wall Street Journal*, New York, 3 August 1992.
10. *El Nuevo Herald*, Miami, 23 February 1992.
11. *El Nuevo Herald*, Miami, 14 February 1992. The terrorists in question were Mario Chánes and Ernesto Díaz Rodríguez. The latter, already freed and closely linked to the CANF, undertook tours of Europe organised by the NGO Pax Christi Holland at the end of the 1990s.
12. *Diario Las Américas*, Miami, 5 February 1992.
13. *Diario Las Américas*, Miami, 5 February 1992.
14. *The Wall Street Journal*, New York, 16 October 1992.
15. *El Nuevo Herald* and *Diario Las Américas*, Miami, 26 September 1992.
16. Encinosa, Enrique, *Cuba en guerra*.
17. *El Nuevo Herald*, 28 September 1992.
18. Ibid.
19. In a resounding victory for the Cuban government, 59 countries, including Spain, France, Canada, Mexico and China, condemned the Act at the UN. Three voted in favour: the US, Israel and Romania. There were 71 abstentions, including Russia, Germany and the UK.
20. Vargas Llosa, Álvaro, *El Exilio Indomable*.

CHAPTER 10

1. Televised audience, also in *The Times*, 20 February 1995.
2. Warde, Ibraim, 'Coupes claires dans l'aide extérieure', *Le Monde Diplomatique*, Paris, November 1995.
3. Halimi, Serge, 'Des médias en tenue camouflée', *Le Monde Diplomatique*, Paris, March 1991.
4. Kiger, Patrick and Kruger, John, 'Squeeze Play'. As an illustration of the obsession of the US Congress with the subject: during the 150 sessions held between 1997 and 1998 47 bills concerning Cuba were presented, almost all of an anti-Cuban nature.
5. Ibid. The legislators who finally sponsored the bill in the House were: Dan Burton, Benjamin Gilman, Ileana Ros-Lehtinen, Lincoln Díaz

Balart, Robert Torricelli and Robert Menéndez; and in the Senate: Jesse Helms, Paul Coverdeli, Fred Thompson, Olympia Snowe and Charles Robb.

6. Ibid.
7. Ibid.
8. *Washington Post*, Washington, 12 September 1995. In a report prepared on behalf of the Pentagon it was concluded that Cuba presented no military threat to US security. However, the report also concluded that to try to foment civil war would be a threat due to the potential consequences for the region. *The military and the Cuban transition: a reference guide to policy and crisis management*, Pentagon report, edited by Nestor Sánchez, Washington, March 1995.
9. Letter reproduced in *Diario Las Américas*, Miami, 12 March 1995.
10. Kiger, Patrick and Kruger, John, 'Squeeze Play'.
11. *Diario Las Américas*, Miami, 2 April 1995.
12. *El Nuevo Herald*, 13 May 1995. Orlando Bosch, who maintained close links with the Bacardí magnate's RECE organisation, was declared one of the Continent's worst terrorists by the FBI. After completing his prison sentence in Venezuela as a result of the bombing of a Cubana aircraft in 1976 the US authorities attempted to deport him. The lobby mounted on his behalf amongst the highest political echelons by the Foundation (including President Bush), together with the fact that no other country would accept him, culminated in his arrival in Miami and subsequent freedom. The Cuban government requested his extradition for trial but this was refused. Another organisation that mounted protests was the Cuban Patriotic Committee, which unites the most vociferous of the exiled groupings and grouplets, including the Cuban American National Foundation and which aims to create 'the just and necessary war for Cuba'.
13. *El Nuevo Herald*, 13 May 1995.
14. Kiger, Patrick and Kruger, John, 'Squeeze Play'.
15. Encinosa, Enrique, *Cuba en guerra*.
16. Emilio Estefan Jr is a Bacardí shareholder (Estefan Enterprises, Inc., Miami). For twelve years Emilio worked for Bacardí as the director of marketing for Latin America. Gloria Estefan made her first public appearance in a small Miami nightclub called 'Bacardí' in 1975, accompanied by a small band under Emilio's direction. The singer's father, one time bodyguard of the ex-dictator Batista, was a member of the 2506 Brigade of mercenaries.
17. *Diario Las Américas*, Miami, 21 June 1994.
18. 'Interview with José Basulto' from *Dissidents or Mercenaries? The Cuba Exile Movement*, Calvo Ospina, Hernando and Declercq, Katlijn.
19. *La Jornada*, Mexico, 13 March 1996.
20. Ibid.
21. Altozano, Hermenegildo, 'Spain must protect her investments in Cuba', *El País*, Madrid, 3 June 1996.
22. Kiger, Patrick and Kruger, John, 'Squeeze Play'.
23. 'Tribute to Aznar: in conversation with an exile', *El Nuevo Herald*, 28 November 1995.

CHAPTER 11

1. *El Nuevo Herald*, Miami, 15 July 1995.
2. *Miami Herald*, Miami, 15 July 1995.
3. *Diario Las Américas*, Miami, 19 April 1995.
4. *El Nuevo Herald*, Miami, 15 July 1995.
5. Ibid.
6. *The Sun*, Baltimore, 22 May 1995.
7. *El Nuevo Herald*, Miami, 19 July 1995.
8. Kiger, Patrick and Kruger, John, 'Squeeze Play'.
9. *El Nuevo Herald*, Miami, March 1996.
10. Vargas Llosa, Álvaro, *El Exilio Indomable*.
11. Ibid. As the text makes clear, Bacardí did not create an extensive lobby in the US Congress. Lobbying was undertaken by the Cuban American National Foundation. One of those charged with undertaking what little lobbying Bacardí undertook with the legislators was Luis Aguilar León. In May 1996 Bacardí 'paid [him] emotional tribute for his long and brilliant career as academic and journalist'. Manuel J. Cutillas congratulated him in person. Also present, in addition to other company directors, were the directors of the Cuban American National Foundation Pepe Hernández, Domingo Moreira and Roberto Suárez, as well as Carlos Alberto Montaner (*Diario Las Américas*, June 1996. See photo in Annex II). Montaner, a Cuban exile resident in Spain, is a CIA agent according to the Cuban authorities.
12. Ibid.
13. See the diagram in the Appendix.
14. *El Nuevo Herald*, Miami, March 1996.
15. Ibid.
16. *The Sun*, Baltimore, 22 May 1995.
17. *El Nuevo Herald*, Miami, March 1996.
18. Kiger, Patrick and Kruger, John, 'Squeeze Play'.
19. Vargas Llosa, Álvaro, *El Exilio Indomable*.
20. From 1976 to 1981 Reich was head of the Washington office of the Council of the Americas, an association of US companies with investments in Latin America and the Caribbean and which included Bacardí. He then spent two years in the Latin American section of the US Agency for International Development (USAID), where he resolutely vetoed every request for aid made by the Sandinistas. In turn Ronald Reagan named him US ambassador to the UN in Geneva, a post he accepted with alacrity, as in his own words, 'It is a great honour to represent the United States' (*El Nuevo Herald*, Miami, 28 February 1991). During his tenure at this global body he opened many doors for the CANF and its lobbying efforts against Cuba. Reich is a director of Freedom House together with Kirkpatrick, Malcolm Forbes Jr, Revel, Doherty and others.
21. Another important director of the Brock Group is James Frierson, co-ordinator of US policy towards the implementation of the GATT (General Agreement on Tariffs and Trade) system at the Uruguay talks from 1987–89.

22. *The World of Bacardí-Martini.*

CHAPTER 12

1. This growth has come about in spite of being denied access to the huge US market, a veritable redoubt defended by Bacardí. This is also the source of the intense political activity waged by the rum empire against the lifting of the blockade or even just the resumption of commercial links between the United States and Cuba.
2. Benes, Alejandro, 'The Spirit of the Bat', *Cigar Aficionado*, Washington, 1996.
3. *El libro de Cuba*, Havana, 1925.
4. The World Organisation for Intellectual Property Rights (WOIPR) is a United Nations organisation with its headquarters in Geneva which is responsible for maintaining copyright and intellectual ownership rights. It was created to ensure that the provisions laid down in the Berne (copyright) and Paris (business ownership rights) Conventions be observed, in addition to numerous other special accords adopted within the last of these, in particular the Patents Treaty for Co-operation (PTC).
5. In July 2001, trade unions and human rights groups in Miami began legal proceedings against Coca-Cola for allegedly failing to prevent Colombian bottlers from contracting death squads to repress trade union organisers there. Among the alleged methods used against trade unionists in Colombia are torture and assassination.

CHAPTER 13

1. Malcolm Forbes, owner of *Forbes* magazine, has been chairman of the executive committee of the Committee for Cuban Reconstruction, a body set up by the Cuban American National Foundation (see Chapter 14).
2. *El País*, Madrid, 27 June 1999.
3. Ibid.
4. Ibid. In Spain Bacardí-Martini and the Arechabala family have lodged a claim against the Havana Club Holding Corporation asking for the return of the brand name. The legal firm of Gómez, Acebo and Pombo are acting as lawyers in the case. This firm is a member of the American Corporate Club, whose honorary president is the US ambassador to Spain. The firm's adviser in the claim is Oscar Garibaldi, lawyer for Covington and Burling, a company employed by Bacardí which took part in the drafting of the Helms-Burton Act.
5. 'Declaration made by the Cuban delegation to the TRIPs' Committee', Geneva, 21 April 1999.
6. The main US critics of Section 211 argue that the way in which it was adopted is against the 'ethic' that the US itself would wish to see adopted in such matters. The Alexis de Tocqueville Institute, a Washington think tank known for its defence of intellectual property rights, called

on Congress to repeal Section 211 on the grounds that it violated WTO conventions. The section was not debated by either house. The president of the Institute, Kenneth Brown, knowing that Bacardí-Martini is one of the biggest contributors to political campaigns, said that 'finally one gets the impression that some members of Congress use their legislative powers in order to satisfy the special interests of their contributors'. Pruzin, Daniel, *BNA Inc. Daily for Executives*, 12 June 2001.

7. The panel (group of experts) of the World Trade Organisation (WTO) confirmed that Section 211 is in contradiction with the obligations of the United States as regards protection and respect for intellectual property. In this sense it supported the European Union, which maintains that the section denies the owners of Cuban commercial trademarks access to American courts in order defend their intellectual property rights. If the United States permits it, and it is their obligation, the European company Pernod-Ricard, which is contesting on behalf of the Franco-Cuban Pernod-Ricard–Havana Club Holding, could make the demand for their ownership of the trademark of Havana Club Rum. If the United States respects the decision of the WTO, their Congress should abolish that law and allow the trademark to continue to be registered in the name of the holding. Therefore the Arechabala family cannot continue insisting on the ownership of the trademark in the United States after having renewed their registration, as required by international norms. What is left outside the proceedings is the sale of the registration of the trademark by the family to the transnational Bacardí under the protection basically of Section 211. Surprisingly, neither the United States nor Bacardí have commented on the verdict of the WTO. Although the decision of the WTO took place in August 2001, and the involved parties may present comments, it is very unlikely that it will be changed.

CHAPTER 14

1. 'For a Free and Democratic Cuba'.
2. Betancourt, Ernesto, 'La solución interna' (The Internal Solution), *El Nuevo Herald*, Miami, 13 September 1991.
3. Author's italics (ed.).
4. *Miami Herald*, Miami, May 1994.
5. 'Brilliante cierre del Congreso Hemisférico' (Brilliant climax to the Hemisphere Congress), *Diario Las Américas*, Miami, 24 September 1991.
6. Caroit, Jean Michel 'A Panamá, de "justes causes" toujours en attente de solution', *Le Monde Diplomatique*, Paris, January 1991.
7. *Diario Las Américas*, Miami, 19 and 30 April 1994.
8. Except where credited otherwise, all information quoted regarding the aims of the Business Council have been taken from their own published documents (www.us-cubabusinesscouncil.org/ www.uscubabiz.org/).
9. *El Nuevo Herald*, Miami, 13 July 1995.
10. Cuba On-Line, set up towards the end of the 1990s, is designed to provide information and various types of analysis on Cuba to companies and corporations interested in investing following the demise of the

current political system. In 1999 USAID made a contribution of $300,000. Among its most important directors are the highly placed Bacardí executive Juan Prado and the ex-CIA and Pentagon employee Nestor Sánchez who was implicated in an assassination attempt on Castro in 1963. Bacardí uses Cuba On-Line's services.

11. Since 1970, informal gatherings have been held in the Swiss town of Davos, attended by the political heads of the major capitalist powers, in addition to some 900 hundred banking chiefs and heads of global multinationals, including those from Bacardí. The principal topics are: to assess the progress of the market economy; the abolition of all state regulations that stand in its way; and to decide on a global economic strategy. The Davos Summit has become the centre of ultraliberalism and of the single-track theory which postulates the primacy of the domination over society and nation states by capitalism. Although still relatively small, an alliance is taking shape against this summit, especially in Europe, along with social movements such as the Landless Movement in Brazil.

12. Benes, Alejandro, 'The Spirit of the Bat'.
13. Ibid.

Index

126   Bacardí

About the Cuba Solidarity Campaign (CSC)

The Cuba Solidarity Campaign works in the UK to raise awareness against the illegal US economic blockade of Cuba and defends the Cuban people's right to self-determination. It calls upon the US government to open and maintain complete diplomatic and trading relations with the island. CSC also organises public events, annual work brigades to Cuba, sends material aid to the Cuban health and education services and disseminates information explaining the reality of the situation in Cuba.

CSC is a non-party political, non-profit making organisation which depends entirely upon subscriptions, events, sales and donations for its income. Membership is open to individuals and organisations and includes a subscription to *CubaSí*, a quarterly magazine which provides accurate information and views about the island.

If you would like to join or learn more about CSC contact the office:

c/o Red Rose Club,
129 Seven Sisters Road,
London,
N7 7QG

Tel: 020 7263 6452
Fax: 020 7561 0191

Email:
office@cuba-solidarity.org.uk

Websites:
www.cuba-solidarity.org.uk
www.cubaconnect.co.uk